BERTOLT BRECHT

ry
ne
es

he
on
tic
rk
he

ed

he

sal

tial
ge
nt.

at

Meg Mumford is a lecture at
The University of New South Wales, Australia. She has published widely
on the subject of Brecht's theatre and contemporary appropriations of
his theory and practice

ROUTLEDGE PERFORMANCE PRACTITIONERS

Series editor: Franc Chamberlain, University College Cork

Routledge Performance Practitioners is an innovative series of introductory handbooks on key figures in twentieth-century performance practice. Each volume focuses on a theatre-maker whose practical and theoretical work has in some way transformed the way we understand theatre and performance. The books are carefully structured to enable the reader to gain a good grasp of the fundamental elements underpinning each practitioner's work. They will provide an inspiring springboard for future study, unpacking and explaining what can initially seem daunting.

The main sections of each book cover:

- personal biography
- explanation of key writings
- description of significant productions
- reproduction of practical exercises.

Volumes currently available in the series are:

BERTOLT BRECHT

Meg Mumford

Routledge
Taylor & Francis Group

LONDON AND NEW YORK

First published 2009
by Routledge
2 Park Square, Milton Park, Abingdon, Oxon OX14 4RN

Simultaneously published in the USA and Canada
by Routledge
270 Madison Ave, New York, NY 10016

Reprinted 2010

Routledge is an imprint of the Taylor & Francis Group, an informa business

© 2009 Meg Mumford

Typeset in Perpetua by
Taylor & Francis Books
Printed and bound in Great Britain by
CPI Antony Rowe, Chippenham, Wiltshire

British Library Cataloguing in Publication Data
A catalogue record for this book is available from the British Library

Library of Congress Cataloging-in-Publication Data
A catalog record for this book has been requested

ISBN13: 978-0-415-37508-5 (hbk)
ISBN13: 978-0-415-37509-2 (pbk)
ISBN13: 978-0-203-88210-8 (ebk)

ISBN10: 0-415-37508-8 (hbk)
ISBN10: 0-415-37509-6 (pbk)
ISBN10: 0-203-88210-5 (ebk)

To Paul, Imogen and Tom.

CONTENTS

FIGURES

ABBREVIATIONS

BBA	Bertolt-Brecht-Archiv
BT	*Brecht on Theatre: The Development of an Aesthetic*
Werke	*Werke: Große kommentierte Berliner und Frankfurter Ausgabe*

ACKNOWLEDGEMENTS

As Brecht himself was keenly aware, collaboration is an important component of creative production. In the case of this book I have received invaluable support from a wide range of collaborators and research institutions. For helping me to bring Brecht's version of theorized practice alive in the contemporary classroom and studio I thank my students and colleagues at the University of Glasgow, Scotland, and at the University of New South Wales (UNSW), Australia, as well as my workshop co-leader at UNSW, Madeleine Blackwell. For giving me the time to reflect both on Brecht's work in its socio-historical context, and on ways of communicating its relevance to Western performance today, I am indebted to the Faculty of Arts and Social Sciences at UNSW, which granted me fruitful periods of teaching release and study leave.

My thanks also to the many people who have helped me to secure permission to publish the playscript extract and images that appear in this book. For permission to reproduce a substantial extract from *The Caucasian Chalk Circle* I thank Claire Weatherhead at A & C Black and Birgit Weber and Susanne Barwick at Suhrkamp. For permission to publish the visual materials in this book I sincerely thank: Hilda Hoffmann, Volker Schnur, Inge Steinert, Bertolt-Brecht-Archiv (BBA), Sächsische Landesbibliothek – Staats- und Universitätsbibliothek Dresden (SLUB), Stadtmuseum Berlin, Suhrkamp, ullsteinbild, and the

Bildarchiv Preußischer Kulturbesitz (bpk). For assistance in the location and reproduction of images I am deeply grateful to: Frau Uta Kohl, BBA; Dr Lothar Schirmer, Stadtmuseum Berlin; Dr Renate Rätz, Archiv Darstellende Kunst, Akademie der Künste; Frau Ilona Weitzel and Frau Petra Dolle, SLUB; Frau Adriane v. Hoop, Suhrkamp; Frau Margret Schulze, ullsteinbild; and Frau Romana Berg, bpk. And last but not least, a warm thank you to my research assistant, Andreas Aurin, whose deft, meticulous and generous liaison work made it possible for me to establish beneficial communication with the many stakeholders involved in the publication of this book's images. Every effort has been made to trace copyright holders in all copyright material in this book. In the case of some photos, the photographer and/or the permission rights holder could not be determined, and in these instances I urge the relevant people to contact me directly. Any omissions brought to my attention will be rectified in future editions.

In addition, my thanks to Franc Chamberlain, Talia Rodgers and John Golder for providing excellent editorial advice and warm encouragement, to Ben Pigott and Judith Oppenheimer for their careful work and patience, and to the other astute readers who have honed my thinking and writing about Brecht, especially David Barnett, Geoffrey Borny, Ted Braun, Steve Giles, Paul Gray, Patricia Mumford-Coutts, Amy Sargeant and Peter Thomson. And finally, heartfelt thanks to my family, the most patient and generous collaborators in this endeavour.

A LIFE OF FLUX

WHICH BRECHT?

Bertolt Brecht (1898–1956) would have been wary of any introduction that presented him as a fixed monolith, rather than acknowl-
edging that there were 'almost as many Brechts as there were people
who knew him' (Lyon 1980: 205). For he was an ever-changing lover
of flux who came to believe that we are contradictory beings, constantly modified by our interactions with the social and material
world, and by the eye of each new beholder. And there have been
many beholders, each with their own stance on this contentious subject. Some describe him as Europe's most famous Marxist playwright,
director and theatre theorist. Or, Germany's answer to Shakespeare,
but with a political twist. Others regard him as a genius who, despite
his unfortunate political credo, remained a poet of eternally suffering
and enduring humanity. Given that Brecht developed a respect for
Marx, Shakespeare and fame he might not have objected to two of
these descriptions. But it is this writer's position that Brecht had little
time for the idea of eternal suffering.

One of the aims of this chapter is to capture the changeful nature
of Brecht's political attitudes and artistic practice and to locate some
of its sources. These include his acute responsiveness to Europe's
tumultuous political landscape between the end of the nineteenth

century and the beginning of the Cold War. In order not just to survive this upheaval, but also to prosper from it, Brecht had to be constantly on the move. Ironically, the sources of instability in his life played a role in fostering its continuities, especially his passion for experimental learning, collaboration and fighting oppression. Faced with immense social upheaval, Brecht's consistent response was to celebrate and attempt to master change. This book places particular emphasis on that attempt because it seeks to explain why Brecht is still a beacon for political performance makers. It could have told a less flattering or even opposing tale. But in an age like ours, where **capitalism** threatens to suppress alternative social models, celebrating the insightful practice of a contestatory voice and his collaborators seems a timely and necessary strategy.

ON THE MAKE: FROM BAVARIA TO BERLIN (1898–1924)

BORN BY THE LECH

'Eugen Berthold Friedrich Brecht' was born in the Bavarian city of Augsburg on 10 February 1898 at 7, Auf dem Rain, in a building flanked by canals of the river Lech. The apartment was noisy, due to the rushing waters and the file cutter's workshop on the ground floor. However tiresome the noise may have been for its inhabitants, its causes – the water and the labourer – provide rich metaphors for a biographer foregrounding Brecht's long-held interest in flux and the cause of the worker. The choice of lodgings probably stemmed from the realities of his father's modest income – Berthold Friedrich was a commercial clerk for the Haindl paper factory. After the birth of Brecht's brother, Walter, the family took up residence in the so-called 'Colony', a group of four-storey houses built by the Haindl founders for the benefit of needy employees. Brecht's father, promoted to company secretary, was in charge of the administration of this social housing, his family privileged with an entire floor to themselves as well as two attic rooms. Unlike the majority of their neighbours, they could afford live-in servants.

The lifestyle of the Brecht family (Figure 1.1) was typical of the bourgeoisie during the reign of Kaiser Wilhelm II (1888–1918), king of Prussia and last emperor of all the states in the German

Figure 1.1 Brecht aged 10 with his father Berthold Friedrich, his mother Sophie and his brother Walter. © Suhrkamp Verlag, Frankfurt am Main, image courtesy of BBA

commonwealth. The work ethic and aspirational energy modelled by Brecht senior, who in 1917 became the managing director for Haindl, informed the career attitude of his sons. By his mid teens Brecht junior was already in hot pursuit of fame as a literary figure and his brother would become a professor in the field of paper technology. The patriarchal and **class** dynamics of the Wilhelminian empire were manifested in the family's strict sexual division of labour – with women relegated to domestic work – and in its observance of class segregation – although the boys played and fought with their working class neighbours, Brecht's grammar school was an exclusively middle class (and macho) experience. During the exile years in Denmark, he would look back scathingly at his ruling class upbringing:

> I grew up as the son
> Of well-to-do people. My parents put
> A collar round my neck and brought me up
> In the habit of being waited on
> And schooled me in the art of giving orders.

> (Brecht 1979c: 316)

When Brecht wrote this poem he had already proved himself a commanding leader, in the best and worst sense. And one whose behaviour throughout his life was characterized by both a condemnation and a continuation of stifling bourgeois habits.

HISTORICIZING INTERLUDE

Now, let's stop this biographical flow for a moment. From the 'Born by the Lech' episode, what have you learned about the author's attitude towards her subject matter? Why do you think she selected that material and organized it in that way? How does her telling of the tale reveal her historical context, her worldview, her politics? And why has she sometimes used the rather strange strategy of referring to herself in the third person and past tense? These are the types of questions Brecht asked when reading any type of expression, history texts in particular. And he would have started asking these questions from the word 'go', interrupting the flow of the narrative with analytical commentary.

Had Brecht read the opening section of this biography he would have quickly grasped the point of the third person references to 'the author', for he used the same distancing strategy in many of his own reflective writings. Through this choice of narrative voice he communicated his interest in analytical observation of one's own position, and in treating the self as historical rather than eternally present. He would also have recognized that, rather than telling a tale of inborn genius, the biographer was seeking to demonstrate how his ever-changing material, social and historical circumstances conditioned his thought – an approach in keeping with his own. Brecht would have noted too how she emphasized the material circumstances and associated thoughts and habits of his family, focusing on their relationship to work, to a bourgeois ethos of self-improvement and social mobility and to class and gender division. And he would have understood the Marxist social class terminology:

- **bourgeoisie**: When Brecht's father became managing director, he joined the ranks of the bourgeoisie, the capitalist owners of merchant, industrial and money capital who in nineteenth-century Europe replaced the land-owning aristocracy as the economic class in control of the bulk of the means of production.
- *petite bourgeoisie*: Prior to Brecht senior's promotion, he belonged to the group of people, like office workers and professionals, who do not own the means of production but may buy the labour power of others (such as domestic servants) or own small businesses, like the file cutter. Brecht would often apply the term to people who had some economic independence but not much social influence, such as white-collar workers and small shopkeepers.
- **proletariat**: At the Haindl paper mill, Brecht's father employed and made company profit from wageworkers, members of the proletariat or industrial working class, whose means of livelihood was to sell their labour to property owners (for further clarification of Marxist class terminology, see Glossary).

As you read on, see if you can spot other features of the biographer's position, including the influence of socialist and feminist thought.

WAR POET: PATRIOT AND REBEL

Even prior to the outbreak of the First World War (1914), Brecht and his grammar school classmates at Augsburg's Royal

Realgymnasium were indoctrinated in a monarchist and militant nationalism. When Germany officially declared war, Brecht was exempted from active duty owing to his heart condition – he suffered heart cramps and palpitations from an early age. Instead, he chose to serve the fatherland through a series of patriotic texts for the local papers. Under the pseudonym 'Berthold Eugen', he praised the Kaiser's leadership, calling for donations to support families who had lost their breadwinner, and eulogizing self-sacrificing German mothers who put their grief for lost sons behind them and devoted themselves to prayers for victory.

Brecht's pathos-laden jingoism was gradually replaced with a sceptical, realist attitude. In keeping with his new, hard-hitting approach, in 1916 he began to use the terse signature 'Bert Brecht'. In June of that year, the critical tone of a school essay brought him close to being expelled. When asked to write about Horace's revered pronouncement *Dulce et decorum est pro patria mori* ('It is sweet and honourable to die for the fatherland'), Brecht replied in combative mode that it was always hard to die, particularly for those in the bloom of their life, and that only the vacuous – and even then, only if they believed themselves far from death's door – could present self-sacrifice as easy. This was a daring statement in a context where many of Brecht's classmates were being sent to military training or into the heart of the fighting, some never to return and others to be maimed for life. In contrast to his brother and peers, Brecht had no desire to be a hero, managing to avoid military service almost until the end of the war.

After completing school in May 1917, Brecht carried out auxiliary war-worker duties as a cleric and gardener, and was later employed as a private tutor. In October he matriculated at the Ludwig-Maximilians University in Munich, taking courses in literature for two semesters, before suddenly transferring to medical studies. There is little evidence that Brecht applied himself to medicine, and in the summer semester of 1921 he failed to sign up for any lectures. It seems likely that Brecht's transferral arose from a need to ensure that if he were conscripted, it would be as a medical orderly rather than as a soldier. As Brecht said to his life-long friend and future scenographer, Caspar Neher, he would rather collect feet than lose them.

From October to January 1919 Brecht worked on a venereal disease ward of a military hospital, which, in keeping with the topsy-turvydom of the times, was erected in the playground of an Augsburg primary school. It was during this period that he wrote the famous, politically explosive poem 'Legend of the Dead Soldier', a scathing parody of the heroic grenadier figure in German literary ballads who rises from his grave and nobly steps back into battle. Brecht turned the literary tradition on its head by presenting the soldier as a stinking corpse, who, on the whim of the Kaiser, is 'resurrected' and declared fit for service by an army medical commission. After pouring schnapps down the soldier's throat, painting over his filthy shroud with the black-white-red of the old imperial flag, and hanging two nurses and a half-naked prostitute in his arms, they parade him through the villages. The next day, as he has been taught, he dies a hero's death. The shocking nature of Brecht's attack on idealized heroism was intensified by the contrast between the grotesque imagery of the lyrics and the gentle and sentimental melody, an oppositional technique that would become a trademark of his epic and dialectical theatre. The satirical force of the ballad, often performed by Brecht to guitar accompaniment, was such that in 1923 it earned him fifth place on the Nazi's list of people to be arrested once they were in power.

Brecht's rebellion against authoritarianism indicates an early interest in power structures, a rebellion motivated at this stage more by a concern with his own empowerment than any revolutionary vision of large-scale social change. The desire to be top dog himself would characterize aspects of Brecht's life-long behaviour, in some cases leading to a perpetuation of invidious power relations. For example, his frequently commandeering and proprietorial treatment of women recalled the habits and double standards of his imperial forebears. At the same time that Brecht was convincing Paula Banholzer – the mother in 1919 of his first child, Frank – to break off her engagement with another man and remain loyal to him, he was pursuing the opera singer Marianne Zoff, soon to become his first wife and mother of his daughter Hanne. Brecht's desire to orchestrate and sustain multiple love relationships at any one time bears some relation to 'his delighted, sometimes obsessive engagement with collective activity' as well as his 'tendency to take the lead in such activity' (Thomson, in Thomson and Sacks, 1994: 23).

Brecht's simultaneous encouragement of 'think-tank' collectives embodied a relatively egalitarian version of this engagement. In Augsburg these groups consisted of a circle of predominantly male friends who often met in Brecht's attic room, where there would be singing and music making, discussion, reading and reciting. From the mid-1920s onwards, working-class and female members – especially lovers – were increasingly represented as co-workers. Brecht spear-headed and led these collectives – a significant number of his plays, including world-renowned texts like *The Threepenny Opera*, *Mother Courage and Her Children* and *The Caucasian Chalk Circle*, were written and researched in collaboration with others. And it was he who basked most in the fame and royalties they brought. Nevertheless, for the majority of participants who chose to be involved, they were exciting and relatively democratic forums where creative productivity was fostered *en masse*.

A SWINE AND HIS CREATURE COMFORTS

The post-war period would not have been an easy time to become a breadwinner, especially if your aim was to forge a career as a poet. Brecht's response to a social context riven by hunger, unemployment and hyperinflation was to assert – both in his private life and through his art – the nature and importance of material needs and survival strategies. His increasingly materialist outlook – the philosophical view that everything that really exists is material in nature and that every-thing mental is a product of phenomena that can be accessed through the senses – was at odds with expressionism, the dominant experi-mental theatre in the early post-war years. The expressionist movement contained diverse and often contradictory tendencies, but many of the playwrights were idealist in so far as they thought non-material mind and spirit were the prime shaping forces of human experience and the world. Their idealism partly explains the so-called 'New Man' figure found in many of their plays, including Friedrich from Ernst Toller's *The Transformation* (1919), a poet-leader who seeks to change the world through visionary speeches that rejuvenate community spirit.

Brecht's play *Baal* is an expression of his irritation with expressio-nist idealism and pathos. The first version of the play – it became customary for Brecht to revise or adapt earlier work in the light of new circumstances – was written in the spring of 1918, within a month of the Munich Chamber Theatre production of Hanns Johst's *The Lonely One*. Energized by his love of opposition, Brecht proclaimed that he could write a better play than Johst's expressionist drama, but the resulting counter play was by no means totally oppositional. For example, both texts are episodic presentations of men experiencing social alienation. And as in other expressionist work, *Baal* depicts a journeying, semi-autobiographical protagonist. Brecht's contestatory attitude, as well as his tendency to preserve aspects of the contested model, remained a hallmark feature of his creative approach. Johst presents his protagonist as a lonely playwright genius, misunderstood by the inferior mass. Baal is also a writer, but he is an earthly hedonist who puts drink, food and sex before his poetry. Rather than being a superior and isolated soul, Baal is an insatiable, desiring body who interacts voraciously, guided purely by his own pleasure and greed for sensual experience with men, women and nature. Unlike Toller's poet-leader, his journeying does not lead to heroic self-transformation. Rather, seemingly worn down by rough living and an asocial existence, Baal simply merges with matter: on a stomach full of stolen eggs, he dies alone in the dirt of a forest.

Brecht's vagabond outsider, Baal, embodies a deep dissatisfaction with imperial Germany. Like his favourite playwright at the time, Frank Wedekind, Brecht's shockingly transgressive expressions constituted a rebellion against duty, conformity and suppression of desire. But the revolt was circumscribed by a focus on his own freedom and notoriety, and an unwillingness to commit to any political agenda for change. While Brecht was immersed in *Baal*, and the pleasures of the local fairground, others were choosing the path of martyrdom in defence of the newly proclaimed Bavarian Republic. During the political chaos after the Kaiser's abdication, left-wing activists – including Ernst Toller – seized the opportunity to oust the king of Bavaria and assert a socialist government. It was declared on 9 November 1918 in Munich by Kurt Eisner, who was the poet-leader of Germany's Independent Social Democrat Party (USPD). In an attempt to ensure grass-roots involvement in government, the Republicans instituted workers' and soldiers' councils. Brecht was elected as a representative for the soldiers' council of the Augsburg military hospital, a role involving tasks such as making reports on soldiers' complaints about everyday matters. Brecht would later praise such dialogic approaches to government, but on this occasion his participation was to be short-lived and unremarkable.

The USPD had been established in 1917 by dissatisfied SPD members. From this breakaway group two mythologized revolutionaries,

Rosa Luxemburg and Karl Liebknecht, established the Spartacists, who by early 1919 were officially the German Communist Party (KPD). Meanwhile, a provisional national government had been formed in Berlin with the SPD leader, Friedrich Ebert, at its helm. In a bid to establish stability, Ebert made a pact with the *Oberste Heeresleitung* (OHL, Supreme Army Command), which stipulated that the government would not attempt to reform the Army if it promised to protect the government. 'Protection' activities included crushing left-wing dissent with the support of right-wing military forces, such as the *Freikorps* – volunteer units trained by the German Army and made up of demobilized (and disgruntled) officers and soldiers. After the KPD went on the assault, occupying the Berlin newspaper quarter and inciting workers to take up arms against the government, the *Freikorps* were sent in and on 15 January 1919 Luxemburg and Liebknecht were brutally murdered. Hot on the heels of this event, Kurt Eisner was shot dead, and government troops, together with the *Freikorps* and a group called the 'white guard', viciously suppressed the Bavarian Republic in both Augsburg and Munich. Its poet-leaders were either executed or imprisoned. In February, after nationwide elections, the first German republic was declared in the city of Weimar. Until 1933, this so-called Weimar Republic would continue to be dominated by the struggle for power between right- and left-wing forces.

Brecht was by no means uninterested in these political upheavals, but he preferred to remain on the sidelines, operating as a critical – but not yet committed – observer. Taking a stance brought with it the threat of personal danger and the possibility of disconnection from friends and family – Brecht's brother and his friend Otto Müllereisert played an active role in the white guard's activities in Munich. Nevertheless, Brecht did make some left-wing gestures, joining the commemorative marches for Eisner and the KPD leaders, writing theatre reviews for the USPD's newspaper, and harbouring Georg Prem, an important member of the Augsburg workers' and soldiers' council.

One of the ways Brecht grappled with the events of 1919 was through the writing of a shockingly unsentimental soldier-returns-home play set during the Spartacist uprising in Berlin. *Drums in the Night* (originally titled *Spartacus*) presents different responses to the uprising, giving particular prominence to the non-heroic attitude of the protagonist, Kragler, a soldier who has just returned after four years service in Africa. At the play's finale, the war-weary Kragler faces a dilemma, being urged by the Spartacists to join the fighting. At the same time he discovers his fiancée is pregnant with another man's child. His uncertainty does not last long. The revolution is quickly dismissed as far less attractive than the opportunity to savour some creature comforts: 'Is my flesh to rot in the gutter so that their idea should get into heaven? ... I am a swine, and the swine's going home' (Brecht 1998: 114–15). According to the actor who played Kragler in the first production, his character's attitude towards the Spartacist cause echoed Brecht's own scornful treatment of the Revolution in both Munich and Berlin as ridiculously incompetent (McDowell 1976: 105).

FAME IN THE JUNGLE OF TWO CITIES

Brecht's sensitivity to a context riddled with violent oppositions and power struggles was reflected in his next play, *In the Jungle* (1922). A dramatization of a fight between two men in the city of Chicago, the play presents the attempt of the Malayan lumber dealer Schlink to take control of George Garga, an impoverished employee of a lending library. When Garga clings to what he calls his freedom, refusing to sell his own opinion of a book, Schlink declares war and a bitter battle ensues in which both protagonists lose their livelihood, Garga his family and lover, and Schlink his life. During a performance of the play on 18 May 1923 at Munich's conservative Residenz Theater, members of the emerging Nazi party staged a protest against its purported glorification of communism by throwing gas bombs into the auditorium. The performance resumed after the smoke had subsided but the production was soon withdrawn. The protestors' interpretation is bemusing, for as Brecht pointed out towards the end of his life, the play 'was meant to deal with this pure enjoyment of fighting' (Brecht 1998: 438) rather than consciously addressing any struggle between ruling and working class.

The crushing of the Bavarian Republic and the increased presence, during the inflation years, of the Nazis and their henchmen, led members of the intelligentsia, including Brecht, to consider leaving both Munich and the country. Brecht first witnessed Nazi pageantry when he attended a Hitler event in June 1923, together with expressionist playwright and friend Arnolt Bronnen. The event proved stimulating but frightening. According to Bronnen, it inspired a night-long musing on a contemporary mass play that would take place in the circus and deal with hunger, inflation and liberation. And the spectacle of masses of wooden, brown-shirted *petit bourgeois* figures brandishing a red flag prompted Brecht to reflect on the unwelcome advent of a Bavarian society born of anarchy, alcohol and a taste for material comfort and nationalist politics. Bronnen found the advent of 'Mahagonny' – Brecht's name for the philistine utopia yearned for by these marching figures – to be a much more inviting prospect (Ewen 1970: 130). In the late 1920s Brecht would distance himself from Bronnen, who became increasingly involved in right-wing and Nazi circles. Brecht was confronted by Nazi theatrics once again in 1923, when he arrived to direct a rehearsal of his play *Edward the Second* at the Munich Chamber Theatre in November and found the actors talking about Hitler's attempt at a military coup in the city. Brecht cancelled the rehearsal and later that day, at a gathering of Jewish and communist friends, discussed the siege and the issue of whether and how long it was wise to remain in Germany. On this occasion, Hitler's beer-hall putsch proved short-lived and rehearsals continued the next day.

Despite – or perhaps precisely because of – his personal experience of right-wing aggression, Brecht continued to keep his distance from off-stage party politics, immersing himself in the world of the theatre. During his second visit to Berlin in the winter of 1921 his efforts to publicize himself and his work brought dividends when, in November 1922, he was awarded the prestigious Kleist Prize for drama. Brecht also applied himself to learning the trade, observing the work of famous expressionist and post-war directors Karl-Heinz Martin and Leopold Jessner, and gaining entry to rehearsals of August Strindberg's *The Dream Play* under the direction of Max Reinhardt, one of the most prolific and influential impresarios in the German-language theatre. Many of the following performance methods, which Brecht witnessed, would later feature in modified form in his work:

- vivid gestures and diction;
- self-conscious theatricality;
- emblematic use of actors and audio-visual imagery to denote ideas;
- group choreography, tableaux and chorus.

These approaches proved easily transferable to what became his trademark – a theatre concerned with the lucid and critical demonstration of social attitudes and relations.

The cabaret scene in both Munich and Berlin was another formative training ground. Throughout the 1920s Brecht made appearances as a cabaret performer, pretending to be a clarinettist in a sketch called *Orchestra Rehearsal* by the Bavarian folk comedian Karl Valentin (Figure 1.2) and impressing audiences with demonic renditions of songs like 'Legend of the Dead Soldier' at a Berlin cabaret called The Wild Stage. On 30 September 1922 he even tried his hand at organizing a one-off midnight revue called 'The Red Raison', at the Chamber Theatre. This cabaret's 'mix of popular entertainers, stage actors and "authors," all of whom are personal acquaintances performing for the fun of it' was exactly the type of event Brecht loved (Calandra 1974: 87). While Brecht's participation in different types of cabaret came to an end at the close of the 1920s, many of their defining ingredients, outlined below, had an enduring impact on his work:

- an episodic structure characterized by self-contained parts;
- the mixing of 'high' (e.g. poetry) and 'low' (e.g. music hall) art;

Figure 1.2 Brecht as cabaret performer in a sketch called *Orchestra Rehearsal*, May 1920. Brecht is flanked by Karl Valentin and his partner comedian, Liesl Karlstadt. Image courtesy of BBA

- separation of actor from character;
- defamiliarizing parody;
- overt engagement with the audience;
- satirical engagement with society.

His exposure to cabaret and comedic performers, especially Valentin on stage and Charlie Chaplin on screen, certainly strengthened his knowledge of comic devices and their usefulness for puncturing the familiar world and engendering pleasurable critical distance. Valentin also gave Brecht advice about how to help actors become gestural demonstrators, and in this respect Brecht had much to learn.

Like many directors, Brecht began as an authoritarian figure, only gradually moving towards the role of a dialogue partner. His first attempt – a Berlin production of Bronnen's *Vatermord* – came to an abrupt end in April 1922 when the star actors abandoned the project out of frustration with his alienating tendency to forge a new performance mode by simply tearing apart the one they were comfortable with. These actors were well versed in the art of carrying the audience away with their charismatic and passionate performances, and Brecht wanted none of it. But at this stage he did not know how to create the different performance mode he had recently begun to articulate in his diary, one where the spectator 'is not fobbed off with an invitation to feel sympathetically, to fuse with the hero' but enjoys 'a higher type of interest to be got from making comparisons, from whatever is different, amazing, impossible to take in as a whole' (Brecht 1979b: 159). Despite his inexperience, Brecht was given the post of dramaturge and director at the Chamber Theatre in the autumn of 1922. It was during his first assignment as named and independent director of one of his own plays, the *Edward the Second* production of March 1924, that he started to make headway with a new mode of realist performance.

John Fuegi has referred to this performance mode as a mixed or contradictory mimetic style (Fuegi 1987: 36), wherein Brecht would combine careful imitation of social actuality, in the manner of Stanislavsky with a playful, defamiliarizing depiction or distortion. For example, in *Edward*, the actors playing the soldiers who prepare to hang the rebel Gaveston were given a working gallows and instructed to copy the details of a hanging so precisely that they would look as if they regularly carried out such work. They were to perform these actions against an ostentatiously askew and painted canvas backdrop and in 'whiteface' make-up, signifying, perhaps, their state of fear and fatigue during battle (Fuegi 1987: 24, 33). The end product was a tense unity of elements from (a) the late nineteenth-century naturalism that dominated mainstream theatre in Augsburg and even permeated expressionist stagings and (b) popular non-realist forms such as could be found in cabaret and fairground shows. The mixed mimetic staging reflects Brecht's life-long interest in both imitating concrete reality – e.g. the exploited underling henchmen – and making strange their socialized behaviour and its social causes, in this case the soldiers' submission out of habit, fear or exhaustion. The mixing of styles was coupled with a dialogic approach to the creation of both play and production. Not only was *Edward* co-authored with Lion Feuchtwanger, but Brecht encouraged cast, crew and casual spectators to attend the rehearsals and welcomed suggestions, constantly changing his text in the light of the new ideas and bodies before him. Having established the cornerstones of his later directorial style during the 1924 production, Brecht then set off to forge new collectives in Berlin, where he had secured the position of dramaturge at Reinhardt's Deutsches Theater.

CHANGING THE WORLD: WEIMAR POLITICS (1924–33)

FROM PUGILISM TO CLASS STRUGGLE

During the mid to late 1920s in Berlin, Brecht began to develop a theatre of social commentary and to use the term 'epic' to describe it. Early **epic theatre** had much in common with the other art forms that accompanied Germany's economic stabilization. Due to events like the rescheduling of war reparation payments in 1924, the country could once again focus on industrial productivity. The obsession with maximizing output encouraged an 'attitude that sought to apply the engineering principles of rationality and streamlining to all aspects of life' (Rosenhaft in Thomson and Sacks 1994: 14). One embodiment of this attitude was *Neue Sachlichkeit* ('New Objectivity' or 'New Sobriety'), a structure of feeling and type of artistic expression char-acterized by an emphasis on sober observation, utility and clarity. Art forms associated with this aesthetic included documentary-style plays dealing with topical issues; the detective novel (Brecht himself was a fan of the crime thriller); and the clear and satirical representations of corrupt society by the visual artist Georg Grosz, who became a member of Brecht's circle. In the late 1920s Brecht would describe New Objectivity as both a necessary advance and an ultimately reactionary affair (*BT* 17), presumably because its emphasis on rational argumentation and intensified productivity as the means for alleviating social inequality was not combined with an understanding of the need to dismantle capitalism. However, its treatment of society as an object for critical reflection had a lasting impact on his approach to the issue of how the artist and spectator should look at their work and world.

Throughout the 1920s, Brecht's interest in a critically distanced way of looking was overtly connected with a macho assertion of masterful wit, one that expressed itself in his tough-boy posturing, complete with Caesar haircut, leather jacket and phallic cigar. Inspired by popular cultural events like music hall, where the patrons (often predominantly male) could smoke and drink while watching, Brecht began to promote the image of a smoker's theatre of relaxed and therefore discerning 'cool' spectators who would not be 'carried away' by the on-stage world. He lauded sports events – expansive bright lighting and a lack of mystery and suggestion – as another example of how to set the scene for shrewd spectatorship. Of all the sports that constituted post-war Germany's major entertainment spectacles, it was boxing that most inspired the non-athletic Brecht. One of the members involved in Brecht's next collective venture, the play *Man is Man*, was a proficient boxer who had acted as a second to the heavyweight champion Paul Samson-Körner. Brecht began working on a biography of the champion in early 1926 but it was never completed (Figure 1.3). Boxing matches contained both a clear demonstration of a skilled struggle for survival and a critical audience. Brecht invoked the boxing model frequently in this period, even using a roped platform recalling the boxing ring in his production of *The Measures Taken* (1930), a play that contains no overt references to the sport. It stages a type of court trial, encouraging both on- and off-stage audiences to judge the behaviour of a Young Comrade, whose tendency to act impulsively in accordance with his emotions endangers the collective. Brecht's treatment of boxing and sport spectatorship is marked by some intriguing blind spots. For example, he fails to address the passionate and empathetic nature of the onlookers,

Figure 1.3 Brecht with Paul Samson-Körner. © ullsteinbild

perhaps a symptom of his tendency at this time to dismiss illusionist theatre as effete, and his longer-term interest in art that minimized emotional enthralment.

The figure of the boxer, a complex icon in Weimar culture, was used to celebrate both the mechanized and trained body, as well as the primitive heroic warrior who fights to reassert himself in the age of the machine and mass living (Bathrick 1990). These contradictory responses reflected an ongoing anxiety about the large-scale shift from rural to industrial city life that dominated the early twentieth century. Urbanization, together with the impact of late nineteenth-century thinkers, such as Darwin, Freud and Marx, intensified debates about the nature of man and the relation of the individual to the collective. Brecht waged a long and unresolved struggle with some of these contemporaneous issues during the copious rewriting and staging of *Man is Man*. Ideas for a play about human identity date back to 1918, but it was not until the formation of the so-called 'Brecht collective' in the mid-1920s – an ever-changing team of artistic collaborators – that the title and overall shape emerged. The version of the grotesque comedy that was premiered in September 1926 uses the image of a trained fighter (a soldier) to explore the malleable nature of man and his exchangeability. Its protagonist, a poor, Chaplinesque Irish dock-porter called Galy Gay, is transformed by a group of British soldiers in a mythical Indian Kilkoa into their missing team mate, Jeriah Jip. After a quick lesson in how to use his weaponry, Gay-cum-Jip becomes a bloodthirsty fighting machine that single-handedly guns down a fortress blocking the British army's pass into Tibet.

In a radio talk of 1927, Brecht suggested that, far from mourning the loss of personality in a technologized mass, *Man is Man* actually celebrated man's malleability and his empowerment through the collective. However, it is hard to reconcile Brecht's positive appraisal of Gay's transformation with the fact that, not only does Galy Gay acquiesce to the lackeys of an imperial army, but his initially fluid self becomes locked in the patterns of a machine-like killer (Schechter in Thomson and Sacks 1994: 73–4). When Brecht directed the play in 1931, the alarming growth in political power of the Nazis spurred him to emphasize the brutality of the collective that his protagonist is all too easily persuaded to join. According to Brecht's friend the Soviet playwright Sergei Tretiakov, the clown-like soldiers were depicted with distinctly sinister overtones, 'armed to the teeth and wearing uniforms caked with lime, blood and excrement', two of them stalking about the stage on stilts and a third padded out in a grotesque manner (Tretiakov, in Brecht 1979a: xiii) (Figure 1.4). When revising the play in 1954, Brecht reinterpreted its theme as 'the false, bad collectivity (the "gang") and its powers of attraction', locating the appeal of Nazism for the *petite bourgeoisie* in their longing for a 'genuinely social collectivity of the workers' (Brecht 1979a: 108).

Figure 1.4 Man is Man, Berlin 1931, with Wolfgang Heinz (left), Alexander Granach and Theo Lingen (right) as soldiers. © ullsteinbild

MEETING MARX

Brecht's understanding of the nature of the individual and the quality of the collective was greatly influenced by his Marxist studies, which began after the Darmstadt premiere of *Man is Man* in autumn 1926. His decision to read Marx's *Capital* was triggered by his difficulties with *Joe Fleischhacker* (1924–9), a play about the demise of a family who leave the country for the big city, only to perish on the streets of Chicago when it is thrown into chaos by the wheat speculations of Fleischhacker. The play embodied Brecht's desire to bring to the stage new and topical subject matter, like stock exchange manoeuvres and economic catastrophes. With the help of Elisabeth Hauptmann, the collaborator and lover working most closely with him at the time, he gathered considerable information. Yet it was not until he began reading *Capital*, Marx's examination of the capitalist mode of production, that the fog surrounding complicated money transactions and the causes of economic crisis began to lift. By the summer of 1927 Brecht was asking the actress Helene Weigel, soon to be his second wife, to send him a stockpile of Marxist literature.

But what became a life-long engagement with a Marxist mode of looking at the world did not translate into a commitment to the German Communist Party. Unlike Hauptmann and Weigel, who joined the KPD in 1929, Brecht never became a card-carrying member. One of his collaborators during the years in America, Hans Viertel, aptly described Brecht's complicated position as that of 'a one-man political party in close coalition with the Communists' (Lyon 1980: 302). Rather than tow the line of a large-scale, pre-established collective, he preferred the role of a supportive but independent observer. Brecht was more at home with smaller-scale think-tanks, like the group who met at his apartment in 1931 to discuss **dialectical materialism** under the guidance of the ex-KPD dissident Karl Korsch.

The centrality of the dialectical idea that contradictions are the source of change and progressive development was one of the key factors that drew Brecht to Marxism. Not surprisingly, given the strife-ridden and rapidly modernizing context in which Brecht lived, he had long been fascinated by contradiction, oppositions and flux. Marxism added a compelling explanation of the nature and causes of individual and social change, and a vision of progressive movement towards a classless society. While the impact of Marxist theory is discussed in Chapter 2, here it is necessary to reflect briefly on its fundamental ideas important to his life work. With regard to the issue of human nature, Marx presented man as both conscious agent and an economically determined object. For Marx, 'humans begin to distinguish themselves from animals as soon as they begin to produce their means of subsistence' and in so doing change themselves and the material world (Marx 1977: 160). However, despite possessing this productive capacity, one that requires consciousness and the ability to cooperate, humans are simultaneously conditioned 'by the social form which exists before they do, which they do not create, which is the product of the preceding generation' (Marx 1977: 192). Following Marx's treatment of determining forces, Brecht's approach to characterization increasingly demonstrated the impact on behaviour of economic class – the roles individuals play in production and in reproductive processes such as childcare and domestic work.

However, while his characters were vividly marked by economic determination, Brecht was wary of presenting them as totally determined or mechanical objects. Brecht's increasing interest in human agency is evident in his teacher-learner characters who transform themselves, such as the revolutionary Pelagea Vlassova, the heroine of *The Mother* (1931), who learns to read and write and then herself becomes a teacher of political intervention. Arguably the most persuasive embodiment of human agency in Brecht's theatre is the practice he developed in the 1930s of an actor who both depicts a character and critically demonstrates that she is a decision-making agent, at any one moment capable of making differing choices. Through the actor-cum-commentator, or **'spectActor'** as it will be referred to, Brecht also found a way of reminding audience members that they, too, are capable of conscious intervention.

Marxist analyses of capitalism and class struggle clarified for Brecht the possibility of positive intervention against social injustice. Marx located capitalism as the most recent but by no means final mode of production; one dominated by the creation and private ownership of capital by the bourgeoisie. He argued that the class struggle between capitalists and exploited proletariat would culminate in a revolution and the emergence of a workers' state. By maintaining the best of capitalism, its productive capacity, and replacing its divisive private property relations with collective ownership, this socialist state would forge a classless communist society and itself eventually wither away.

The type of intervention required to kick-start the revolution remained debated. Brecht's declaration in the mid-1930s, that his epic theatre was for philosophers who 'wished not just to explain the world but also to change it', suggests that the cultivation of a revolutionary consciousness was his preferred mode of intervention (*BT* 72).

PISCATOR AND OTHER REVOLUTIONARY EXPERIMENTS

Of the Berlin practitioners involved in epic art, it was the founder of documentary theatre, Erwin Piscator (1893–1966), who was the most influential in turning Brecht towards an openly political theatre. Piscator's agitational work began with his creation of the Proletarian Theatre in 1920, a no-frills ensemble that toured venues in working-class slums with the aim of developing class consciousness and proletarian solidarity. In 1924 at the Volksbühne he began experiments with new mass-media and narrative forms, translating Alfons Paquet's novel *Flags* into an epic drama by interrupting the flow of action with critical commentary through means such as film, projected texts and direct address to the audience. When Brecht became a member of Piscator's dramaturgical collective in 1927, he gained direct access to the most opulent and technologized phase of Piscator's career, one dependent on a wealthy patron and bourgeois audiences. Brecht also witnessed Piscator's more technologically sparse work when he saw *Paragraph 218*, a touring piece dealing with the contemporary debate concerning the illegality of abortion and aiming to show how the Civil Code oppressed working-class women. In order to animate the audience, Piscator staged semi-improvised dialogues in the auditorium between actors who stood up and spoke about the issues from the point of view of a lawyer, a magistrate, a clergyman and so on, as well as inviting the local doctor to give a speech about the social problems being addressed. Brecht described the show as 'a huge success' (*BT* 66), and no doubt it stimulated his thinking about how to create spectActors in the auditorium as well as on stage.

One of Piscator's innovations was to use the 'living wall' of the film screen and archival voice recordings to tie the events on stage to a wider socio-political reality and to the forces active in history at large. Brecht acknowledged and integrated many of these interruptive and historicizing innovations, particularly in the 1932 production of *The*

Mother. Another trademark of Piscator's theatre was his decentralization of the individual and emphasis instead on his relation to society through methods such as:

- large casts and projected images of mass phenomena;
- the use of groups as the units of action;
- the placement of the actor as merely one among many collaborators.

Brecht developed a similar emphasis on the individual's relation to society, as demonstrated in his focus on:

- the events *between* rather than *within* characters;
- his representation of the collective through the use of choir and chorus;
- his arrangement of large-scale groupings that illuminate social power relations.

However, through his development of gestic acting (see Chapter 2), Brecht would give the actor a much more central role to play in the creation of social commentary. And while Piscator used 'moving' documents and facts about recent history and current affairs, often confronting the audience in a sensational and immediate way, Brecht tended to use characters and events set in more geographically and historically removed contexts so as to encourage comparative and problem-solving responses.

Brecht's love of artistic experimentation and his familiarity, partly through witnessing the work of colleagues like Piscator, with the need to target different audiences and institutional contexts, led him to create a variety of theatre forms. Most of these were *Schaustücke* ('show/showing plays') in that they perpetuated the division between performer and receiver. To varying degrees they also fulfilled the criteria for what Brecht described in 1930 as 'Minor Pedagogy'. That is, they belonged to the transition period before the prophesied socialist revolution and operated within existing mainstream theatres, seeking to expose the shortcomings of capitalist society and activate the audience to become involved in changing it. The box-office hit *The Threepenny Opera* (1928), a collaboration with Hauptmann and the composer Kurt Weill supported by private funding, is an example of a *Schaustück* that has some of the defining features of Minor Pedagogy. Loosely set in the British Victorian era, the operetta plots the business machinations and rivalry of the gangster pimp Macheath ('Mac the Knife') and the beggar king Peachum. Through the depiction of Mac's friendship with the Police Chief, Tiger Brown, it also depicts a symbiotic relationship between the legal system and capitalist business. In a highly entertaining way, the play criticises the commodification of humans under capitalism, a system that encourages humans to exploit the labour of others and even sell themselves. Yet the play does not fulfil all of the Minor Pedagogy criteria, because it does not clarify *how* or *whether* human bestiality can be changed through social intervention. Weill's integration of popular music forms, such as jazz, and the use of performers from music hall and musical comedy was in part an attempt to use popular forms to create a socially useful art and challenge elitist forms like opera. However, the catchy songs, easily taken out of context and sold as records or used as dance and coffee-house music, ended up serving rather than subverting capitalist commodification.

One of the perks of the *Threepenny* money-spinner was that it gave Brecht the space to experiment with non-commercial forms for different audience strata. The **Lehrstück** ('learning-play') that emerged was a revolutionary experiment 'meant not so much for the spectator as for those who were engaged in the performance. It was, so to speak, art for the producer, not art for the consumer' (*BT* 80). In keeping with its name – *Lehre* can mean 'teaching(s)' or 'apprenticeship' – the new text and performance was a type of radical experiential pedagogy. Some of the *Lehrstücke* also came close to meeting Brecht's requirements for a 'Major Pedagogy', a theatre of the socialist future that would remove the divisions between actor and spectator. For example, they were designed to turn receivers into participants within the performance process, and to offer a form of interventionist training. Through copying characters' behaviours – and in some rehearsal situations, correcting behaviour – the participants rehearsed how to think and act rather than how to act a script (Bishop 1986: 274). The *Lehrstücke* were imbued with Marxist philosophy and have often been interpreted – by anti-Marxists in particular – as didactic in a doctrinaire way. Yet Brecht was uneasy with agitational theatre that forced a passive reception of a doctrine, and intended these plays instead to encourage a problem-solving engagement with issues such as the individual's relation to the collective.

The two school operas, *He Who Said Yes* and *He Who Said No* (1930), clarify this approach. The original version of *He Who Said Yes* presents the dilemma posed when a research trip through dangerous terrain is jeopardized by one of its young members. The boy has joined in order to get medicine for his sick mother, but then falls ill himself at a time when the team must negotiate the steep ridge of a cliff face. As it is impossible to carry him through the area, in accordance with custom the boy agrees to his own death. Impressed by a comment from one of the pupils involved in rehearsals at the Karl Marx School in Berlin-Neukölln, that it was not correct simply to follow an old custom, Brecht revised the purpose of the trip. It now became an attempt to secure medicine to combat an epidemic that was threatening both the mother and her township. When the boy says 'Yes' to his death, he is moved by medical necessity, not custom. In accordance with dialectical thinking, Brecht also wrote a counter play, *He Who Said No*, which returns in many respects to the original version of *He Who Said Yes* – where the urgency caused by the epidemic is notably absent – but ends with the boy refusing to sacrifice himself. Instead he asks the group to return with him, on the grounds that their research can wait. Moreover, he asks for the introduction of a new custom – the habit of thinking afresh in each new situation. Brecht intended the plays to be performed together, to offer learners the opportunity to experience the individual's relation to society from very different angles.

THE THEATRE OF ECONOMIC AND POLITICAL CRISIS

Brecht's assertion of reasoning behaviour through the *Lehrstücke* was itself a counter play to the Nazis' use of emotive rhetoric and physical force during the chaos of the Great Depression. After the Wall Street crash on 29 October 1929, American investors began withdrawing their loans to Germany and the national stock exchanges plummeted, with the result that industry and foreign trade were crippled. During the course of 1930 unemployment rose to three million and, in March of that year, disagreements about the unemployment programme brought the coalition government to its knees. Turmoil in the Weimar government led to the success of its staunchest opponents, the Communists and the Nazis, in the September Reichstag elections. The increased appeal of the KPD lay in their ability to offer an explanation for the Depression and to characterize it as a symptom of the collapse of capitalism. In their powerful play *St Joan of the Stockyards*, the Brecht collective presented a compelling Marxist interpretation of economic crisis. Marx's theory of the recurrent cycle of modern industry and its stages – end of prosperity, overproduction, crisis, stagnation, restoration – is artistically expressed through the play's narration of how the Chicago meat-packer king, Pierpont Mauler, triggers a crash in the stock market (Völker 1979: 152, 156). The play also presents religion and capitalism as partners in crime. Mauler's relationship with the Salvation Army lieutenant, Johanna Dark, shows how the charity aggravates rather than alleviates the plight of the Depression victims it seeks to serve, both by supplying industrial philanthropists with a good name and by giving little people a security blanket that deters them from political revolt. A selection of scenes from *St Joan* was broadcast on radio in April 1932, but during the Weimar Republic it never reached the public domain again, for, despite the acknowledgment of its quality by reputable directors, no theatre establishment dared stage it.

The following month, a heavily censored version of *Kuhle Wampe* was screened in Germany – a semi-documentary film by the Brecht collective on the subject of the Depression. The film is one example of the way the collective depicted both passive and active responses to class oppression in the hope of stimulating a revolutionary consciousness. Set in Berlin and Kuhle Wampe, its peripheral tent city for workers, it deals with the topical issue of how certain working-class groups 'accommodate themselves in a tired and passive way to the "swamp"' (Brecht 2001: 207). To this end it depicted, for example, the suicide of an unemployed youth who 'never finds his way to the workers' militant struggle and who is driven to death by the cutbacks in unemployment assistance'. By contrast, the third part of the film triumphantly depicts workers' athletics competitions that 'take place on a mass scale and are brilliantly organized' (Brecht 2001: 205).

This opposition of negative and positive models *within* a play or film was often also created *between* plays. For example, if *The Measures Taken* provides an instance of a Young Comrade who learns too late how to be a successful revolutionary fighter, its counter play *The Mother* provides an example of an aged, illiterate and politically reactionary mother of a Russian factory worker, who transforms herself into a communist activist, helping pave the way for the 1917 revolution. The Russian setting was designed to assure 'convinced communists by reminding them that revolution was possible' and to encourage 'unaligned spectators to realize the similarities between the Weimar Republic and Tsarist Russia' (Bradley 2006: 31). For example, scene 5's depiction of soldiers opening fire on a peaceful demonstration against wage cuts in 1905 can be read as a thinly veiled reference to the state brutality Brecht witnessed with his own eyes in Berlin on 1 May 1929, when demonstrating workers were shot down by the SPD's police. Brecht's outrage at 'Bloody May' seems to have strengthened his commitment to a partisan theatre for the oppressed, one that seeks to move (and divide) its participants by appealing to both their rational and emotional faculties.

A more humorous act of state oppression took place on 29 February 1932 at a performance of *The Mother* in the working-class district of Moabit. Due to uproar from some quarters over the play's attack on SPD reformist politics and its seeming call for an uprising, the Theatre Department of the Building Police tried to put a stop to the performance claiming, for example, that it constituted an unacceptable fire risk. The company, including Weigel as Vlassova and amateur performers such as Brecht's future collaborator and lover, Margarete Steffin, then decided to perform without set and costumes. The authorities responded by repeatedly interrupting the performance and limiting what the cast could do (Bradley 2006: 54). Apparently the audience found the event very entertaining, possibly because it confirmed the play's political arguments about oppressive state intervention and heroic resistance.

Unfortunately for Brecht and his co-workers, it was the Nazi state that benefited most from the idea of incendiary communists. Although the Nazis lost a considerable number of votes in the elections of November 1932, their political future was secured when President Hindenburg appointed Hitler chancellor on 30 January 1933. After the burning of the Reichstag on 27 February, for which a Dutch communist was – rightly or wrongly – convicted, Hitler seized the opportunity to suspend civil liberties and to arrest communist leaders. The following day Brecht, Weigel and their two children began an orchestrated flight to Vienna, where Brecht was to give a reading of selected works. It would be sixteen years before Brecht returned to live again in Germany.

ON THE RUN: EXILE IN EUROPE AND AMERICA (1933–47)

FIGHTING THE FEAR AND MISERY OF FASCISM

For Brecht's family, and many of their friends and collaborators, the long exile years were a period of financial deprivation, isolation and uncertainty. Brecht's experience of the trauma of exile and fascism is movingly expressed in his poem 'To those Born Later' (c. 1937–9):

> You who will emerge from the flood
> In which we have gone under
> Remember
> When you speak of our failings
> The dark time too
> Which you have escaped.
> For we went, changing countries more often than our shoes
> Through the wars of the classes, despairing
> When there was injustice only, and no rebellion.

> (Brecht 1979c: 319–20)

The experience of having to work and live in numerous countries in relatively quick succession – Switzerland, France, Denmark, Sweden, Finland, America – and the need to respond to a diverse range of positions on both European fascism and Soviet communism, strengthened Brecht's strategic ability to create a variety of revolutionary theatre forms for different contexts.

Horrified by the Nazification of their fellow countrymen, and deeply disappointed by Stalin's regime, many émigrés lost their faith in the communist project. By contrast, Brecht remained committed to Marx's idea that, through class struggle, the oppressive capitalist mode of production could and would be replaced. This conviction partly explains why, despite his criticism of Stalin's dictatorship and violent use of force, he continued to praise the Soviet leader for fostering a socialist industry free from private ownership. Brecht's emphasis on economic structures also underpinned his rejection of any essentialist explanations of the Nazi phenomenon, such as the idea that it sprang from eternal barbaric impulses, or that the rise of Hitler demonstrated the inherent servitude of the German people. Instead he interpreted fascism as a type of rule that will occur under monopoly capitalism, one that arises when capitalism reaches a point of crisis and can no longer effectively govern by means of parliamentary democracy. Hence, in the 1934 version of the satirical parable play *Round Heads and Pointed Heads*, the Brecht collective presented Nazi racial theory and war-mongering as methods of diverting attention from class division and of stopping the oppressed from uniting in revolt, an interpretation that has been criticized for not fully taking into account the causes and nature of Nazi racism (Ewen 1970: 310). And in the historical farce *The Resistible Rise of Arturo Ui* (1941), Brecht and Steffin drew parallels between the political history of Hitler and the economic history of American gangsters such as Al Capone. For example, they attributed Hitler's seizure of power to the intersection between his *petit bourgeois* aspirations and the willingness of business leaders and landowners to secure market monopolies through gangster terror. The nature of pre-war Nazi terror was expressed vividly by the same authors in *Fear and Misery of the Third Reich* (1938), a loose collection of scenes that movingly demonstrates the atomization of individuals under fascism, the suicidal nature of collusion and the necessity of subversion and mass resistance.

Brecht's attempt to combat fascism by keeping oppositional thoughts alive in difficult circumstances necessitated new modes of operation. For a start, he had to find a substitute for the network of producers he had lost who, literally and figuratively, spoke his own language. On an institutional level this involved making alliances with translators and participating in the founding of ventures such as the anti-fascist German-language journal *Das Wort*, an organ loosely connected with the Soviet-dominated Comintern, an international communist organization dedicated to overthrowing the international bourgeoisie. At the level of creative practice, because his access to theatre institutions was extremely limited, he devoted more time to writing than at any other point of his career, producing a wealth of analytical and lyrical texts and many of the plays canonized in Western theatre, including *Life of Galileo*, *Mother Courage and Her Children*, *The Good Person of Sezuan*, *Puntila and His Servant Matti*, and the play whose spectacular staging is discussed in this book, *The Caucasian Chalk Circle*.

For the first time Brecht's team experimented with work designed primarily to incite immediate political action rather than a long-term change in ways of looking at the world. Thus, in order to make a timely contribution to the united front against fascism, they experimented with theatre methods associated with the bourgeoisie, such as empathetic character–spectator relations. In addition, Brecht grappled with the challenge of engaging audiences that, not unlike contemporary Western spectators, are removed from the type of working class cultural activism that existed in Weimar Berlin. Brecht's experience of new audiences and their theatre traditions, particularly in America, gave him an understanding – though arguably one he failed sufficiently to act upon – of how aspects of local and commercial theatre could be mobilized to help engage audiences in a foreign political theatre of enlightenment. This cultural translation strategy is briefly addressed in the Chapter 3 discussion of the *Chalk Circle*, a play written with musicals and New York's Broadway in mind.

DEFENDING EXPERIMENTAL REALISM

Señora Carrar's Rifles (1937) demonstrates how Brecht and Steffin sought to adapt **Aristotelian** and bourgeois '**dramatic theatre**' techniques (see Chapter 2) so that they served immediate revolutionary ends. The play was commissioned by a company of immigrant actors in Paris who sought to inspire the French workers to continue supporting their comrades in the Spanish Civil War and indict the non-involvement policy of the French and British governments. A feature of this policy was the refusal to supply weapons to the defenders of the legally established Republic of Spain against the fascist General Franco and his war partners, Hitler and Mussolini. The danger of neutrality and the importance of weapons are addressed through the depiction of Carrar's dramatic shift in attitude after she learns that the fascists have shot her elder son gratuitously, while he was fishing in the village harbour. Widow of an Andalusian fisherman who died supporting the Republic, she initially tries to stop her family from becoming involved in violent resistance. At the finale, by contrast, she leaves the stage a gun-toting fighter, using her husband's rifles to arm herself and her fellow republicans.

Señora Carrar diverges from Brecht's earlier epic theatre experiments in several ways. For instance, as in Aristotelian drama, the plot events are smoothly dovetailed rather than arranged in montage fashion with interruptive, defamiliarizing inserts. Moreover, epic breadth and multiplicity are replaced by an Aristotelian preservation of the unities of time, space and action: all the events unfold within Carrar's home while the fictional time frame – the approximately 45 minutes that elapse between her placing a loaf of bread in the oven at the opening and her final exit with both the baked loaf and rifles – corresponds to the length of the play's performance. This dramaturgy encourages the audience to experience the world from the characters' perspectives in an uninterrupted present tense, and to become emotionally involved in Carrar's transformation. However, the overt use of emotional arousal is counterbalanced with a thought-provoking presentation of characters' differing approaches to neutrality. This, together with Brecht's comment to director Slatan Dudow about the simple performance style he envisaged for the piece – 'No hysteria, quiet, well thought-out realism' (Brecht 1990: 258) – testifies to the importance for him of maintaining a space for a reasoning analytical attitude. The end result is a drama that encourages interplay between emotional involvement and reflective observation, a dialectical feature that Brecht would increasingly promote, through both his writing and staging.

The play was very popular with anti-fascist theatre groups and their audiences, due in no small part to the accessible nature of its realism. However, *Señora Carrar*'s indebtedness to a nineteenth-century version of the Aristotelian tradition by no means signalled conversion to a particular (or 'more mature') realist style. Indeed, both before and after this play, the Brecht collective created stylistically diverse works that were 'abnormally disunified in every way. even [*sic*] the genres change constantly. biography, [*sic*] gestarium, parable, character comedy in the folk vein, historical farce' (Brecht 1993: 145). One of the principles underpinning this diversity was Brecht's idea that the stylistic means of realist art should be variable, according to the dictates of time and place. Theoretical reflections of the late 1930s, during a period when realism was hotly debated in Marxist circles, further clarify his commitment to experimentation and his understanding that realist art was a matter of political attitude rather than form (see Chapter 2). This is why he rejected the exclusive promotion of specific bourgeois realist forms by Georg Lukács, a key commentator on Marxist aesthetics and contributor to *Das Wort*, but agreed that realist art should demonstrate the connections between **ideology**, economics and social history (Mumford 2001).

FROM HOLLYWOOD TO THE HUAC INQUISITION

Brecht's sensitivity to the dictates of time and place is clearly manifest in plays such as *Arturo Ui*, written with half an eye to an audience familiar with American gangster history at a time when he was attempting to secure migration visas to the USA. Threatened by the increasing presence of Nazis and their supporters in Finland, Brecht sought refuge in a country where collaborators such as Piscator, Hauptmann and composer-collaborator Hanns Eisler were already based. The Soviet Union was no longer a viable option, for the failure of the German émigré theatre scene and the purging of innovative artists such as Vsevolod Meyerhold and Brecht's friend Tretiakov was proof positive that Stalin's regime would not be a fruitful environment for his experiments. Moreover, the country was on the verge of becoming deeply embroiled in the war. Fortunately, there was still time for the Brecht collective to escape Europe via Russia's shores. On 13 June 1941 Brecht, Weigel, their children, and Brecht's Danish lover-collaborator, Ruth Berlau, set sail from Vladivostok, spirits very much dampened by the loss of their fellow traveller, Steffin, who had died from tuberculosis in Moscow. They eventually entered the harbour of San Pedro, California, on 21 July, only one day before Hitler's army attacked the Soviet Union.

In many respects they had had a lucky escape from Europe. However, during the greater part of the six-year 'exile in paradise', Brecht suffered from a form of cultural shock that left him feeling anything but fortunate. As an experienced man of the theatre, Brecht had developed the art of 'producing' himself, but while living in American exile from 1941 to 1947 'this "production" failed, and his influence passed almost unnoticed' (Lyon 1980: xi). Based in Santa Monica, Los Angeles, where he hoped to earn his keep through scriptwriting for Hollywood, Brecht unwillingly participated in the world of commercial art, where the artist moulds both self and product to suit the industry bosses and their markets:

> Know that our great showmen
> Are those who show what we want to have shown.

Dominate by serving us!
Endure by winning duration for us
Play our game, we'll share the loot
Deliver the goods! Be straight with us!
Deliver the goods.
When I look into their decomposing faces
My hunger disappears.

(Brecht 1979c: 379)

In Brecht's eyes, the showmen of his poem 'Deliver the Goods' (1942) were merely an exaggerated version of the type of citizen produced by a young and capitalist nation. In this automobile-oriented society of rootless mobile workers, where 'houses are extensions of garages' (Brecht 1993: 257), money was the measure of man. Brecht's loss of sales in Europe and his inability to create successful film scripts – with the notable exception of *Hangmen Also Die* (Fritz Lang, 1943) – meant that it was difficult for him to measure up. Ironically, when his financial reserves were particularly low, Weigel had to shop for household goods and clothing in Salvation Army stores, the very charity he had accused of prolonging rather than alleviating the misery of capitalism. One of the reasons Brecht found himself at a loss in the New World was that it did not regard his revelation of how exploitative capitalist business practice governed interhuman relations as a sensational exposure. In his work journal he briefly mused on a historical reason for this attitude, noting that American democracy, unlike its European counterparts, was founded by bourgeois politicians who openly acknowledged their business interests: 'the representatives of the people do not even symbolically have garments without pockets here, as they did in ancient rome [*sic*]' (Brecht 1993: 198).

Brecht's tendency in America was to impose established methods rather than experiment with the traditions of his target audience. This combative response, perhaps fuelled by ideological disdain and pedagogical fervour, first became visible during a visit to America well prior to the period of exile in the 1940s. In the winter of 1934, Brecht travelled to New York in the hope that he could 'influence' a production of *The Mother* by the Theatre Union. His concerns about the show were first triggered by the script. Instead of an agitational, poetic and episodic text that advocated raising class consciousness, particularly of working class women, and revolution as the solution to the crisis of the Great Depression, Brecht discovered a cathartic three-act melodrama in a colloquial American register with revenge tragedy elements. Brecht replaced the adaptation with a stilted, near-literal translation, integrated slides and captions, and persuaded the scenographer to abandon his naturalistic design in favour of a plain structure modelled on Neher's sketches for the Berlin premiere. The final production contained a muddled collision of epic text and setting with illusionistic devices such as empathetic acting – most of the actors were trained in the Stanislavsky-inspired methods introduced to America by the Group Theatre. Unfortunately, it proved an artistic and box-office failure from which the company never recovered. In addition to the stylistic confusion, reviewers panned the didactic elements and their inappropriateness for the Theatre Union's typical audience. While **agitprop** was the official aesthetic of the KPD and a vital tool during the power struggles prior to Hitler's rise, it was not highly regarded in America, where, despite the Depression, the US Communist Party had a relatively minor following and there was no reason to believe revolution was imminent (Bradley 2006: 143). Brecht's involvement in the off-Broadway New York production of *The Private Life of the Master Race* (1945) – an English-language version of *Fear and Misery* – demonstrated a similar lack of inter-cultural dialogue.

By contrast, his approach to the *Life of Galileo* production that premiered in Beverley Hills in July 1947 was characterized by a greater degree of negotiation. One of the factors that made a more dialogic rehearsal process once again possible was the harmonious relationship between the German playwright-director and his leading man, the English actor Charles Laughton. For the first time in America, Brecht was working with a talented performer who, in films such as *The Private Life of Henry VIII* (1933), demonstrated an ability to achieve commentary through gesture. Brecht was particularly fascinated by the scene in the film where Laughton presents the king devouring a chicken, lustily demolishing the bird and throwing the chewed bones behind him, an episode that illuminates, for example, the connection between Henry's material power and his relation to others (his many wives in particular). Laughton was also willing to participate in a lengthy preparation period and a performance that covertly criticised the relationship between contemporary American science and the military.

Mid way through their work, America's involvement in the war took a new direction when, in August 1945, atomic bombs were dropped on Hiroshima and Nagasaki. In response, Brecht further sharpened the new emphases that already informed his work with Laughton. The changes had grown out of Brecht's dissatisfaction with the Denmark version of 1938–39, which explored the control of scientific inquiry by the authorities, especially amid a reign of terror, be it the seventeenth-century Catholic Inquisition of Galileo's Italy or Hitler's regime. What the first version lacked was an unequivocal demonstration that Galileo's recantation of his theories about the solar system had robbed the masses of a revolutionary knowledge, one they could have used to dismantle the theology keeping their rulers in power. Thus, the American version attempted to clarify the belief that Galileo's recantation was a criminal failure of the scientist's responsibility to society, comparable to the placement of atomic research in the wrong hands.

Several reviewers were quick to pick up the critique of modern science and many were willing to engage with the unconventional staging. While Brecht regarded the first version of the play text as 'technically a great step backwards' because of its lack of directness, use of interiors, atmosphere and **empathy** (Brecht 1993: 23), for many in the Hollywood audience this first production was a leap into a new world. For example, reviewers drew attention to the non-illusionist devices, such as the placement before each scene of a verse sung by three choirboys, forecasting the play's events, the use of a boy pulling a gauze sub-curtain across the stage to indicate a change of scene, and the unconcealed movement of props by actors. Despite the fact that other reviewers felt they had been alienated rather than enlightened by the distanciation techniques, Brecht was pleased with the sell-out production.

Shortly after the opening of *Galileo* Brecht was involved in a performance with a very different politics when, on 30 October 1947, he appeared before the US Congressional House Committee on Unamerican Activities (HUAC). After the start of the Cold War in 1946, HUAC initiated a notorious investigation into alleged communist infiltration of the film industry. The announcement of public hearings in Washington sent shock waves through Hollywood, where right and left alike feared that the government was making a bid to control the industry. Eerily, a relationship analogous to that between the scientist Galileo and the state-sanctioned Inquisition threatened to rear its head. Of the many prominent figures summoned, staunch conservatives like Ronald Reagan and Walt Disney proved themselves 'friendly' witnesses by testifying that communists were indeed infiltrating Hollywood. Brecht belonged to the 'Hollywood nineteen', a group who opposed the Committee's inquisitional methods and sought to expose HUAC as violating the American Constitution's First Amendment, guaranteeing freedom of speech and belief. To this end they devised a strategy of fudging the question about Communist Party membership, in the expectation that they would then be able to fight HUAC in the courts for transgressing the Constitution.

Unlike most of 'the unfriendly nineteen', Brecht was in the lucky position of being able to declare that he had never been a Communist Party member. He also argued that the difference between their American citizenship and his 'alien' status meant that it was necessary for him to behave as a guest. Reasons such as these – as well as the desire to safeguard the long-planned and imminent departure to Europe – led him to declare to his comrades that, while he commended their fight for freedom, he thought they should answer the party affiliation question truthfully and oppose the authorities through a show of cooperation that concealed their cunning. Brecht was right to question their mode of resistance – after failure in the Supreme Court, ten of his co-fighters would be sentenced to one year in prison. At his own much-publicized hearing, Brecht gave the most successful strategic performance of his life. Prior to the event he had rehearsed the examination scenario with friends. On the actual day, he arrived dressed up in a respectable dark suit – given to him by a tailor who had worn it at his own wedding – smoked cigars throughout in order to ingratiate himself with the cigar-smoking Head of the Committee, and used an interpreter in order to give himself more time to formulate courteous corrections and cleverly deferent answers to an ill-prepared panel. He was deemed a 'good' witness and let free. The next day he boarded a flight for France. Through their blunders, the investigators had unwittingly supported his cause: 'His departure, planned long in advance, now assumed the form of a dramatic escape from an American witch-hunt. One of the greatest dramatists of the century did not miss the cue' (Lyon 1980: 337).

BUILDING A COLLECTIVE: BRECHT IN THE GDR (1947–56)

A CONTROVERSIAL FIGUREHEAD

Despite his communist sympathies, it would be two years before Brecht set foot in the Soviet-administered zone of Germany. Both the increasing heat of the Cold War and his desire to keep doors open to Europe and its German-language theatres made it extremely difficult for him to find the right address. As a stateless person in the FBI's bad books he was unwelcome in the Western part of Germany governed by the Allies. Moving to the Soviet sector could curtail his travel possibilities, while the emphasis in its cultural policy circles on an anti-Formalist aesthetic posed a threat to his experimental practice. After establishing a new network of collaborators in Switzerland, he and his wife successfully bid for Austrian citizenship, a strategic move designed to allow the possibility of residing in the socialist part of Germany without losing their passports to the world.

During Brecht and Weigel's first visit to East Berlin in October 1948 they were warmly welcomed at a banquet attended by Socialist Unity Party (SED) members such as Wilhelm Pieck – future president of the German Democratic Republic (GDR). The Deutsches Theater was put at their disposal and Brecht began preparing *Mother Courage* for a January premiere, with Weigel playing the title role. This fêted production put Brecht on the East German map as a cultural figurehead, while Weigel's high-calibre performance helped to propel forward her negotiations for a major state-funded company. The result was the famous Berliner Ensemble, for which she secured enough subsidy to sustain over sixty performers, more than 250 associates and lengthy rehearsal periods (Ewen 1970: 458). When the Brechts arrived in Berlin the theatre buildings were allocated already, and thus it would be more than four years before the Ensemble was lodged in Brecht's preferred Theater am Schiffbauerdamm. In the interim they lived cheek-by-jowl with Wolfgang Langhoff's company at the Deutsches Theater. Cohabitation proved difficult, but the Ensemble was fortunate to have the luxury of financial independence from its neighbour, an unusual investment that partly reflected officialdom's faith in the propaganda value of the enterprise. This faith was confirmed at events like the International Festival of Dramatic Art in

Paris, where, in June 1954, *Mother Courage* was judged best play and best production, thereby becoming a flagship for the young socialist state.

However, *Mother Courage* also established the Ensemble's role as a controversial dissenting voice. The heated discussion that surrounded the 1949 staging, a debate spearheaded by Fritz Erpenbeck, editor of a journal influenced by the Party line, made it the first theatre case in the **Formalism** conflicts. Although the term 'Formalism' referred to works which experimented with form for its own sake, it was increasingly used by conservatives in left-wing politics to dismiss any art that deviated from Soviet **Socialist Realism**. The latter, the prescribed artistic practice that emerged from the First Congress of the Union of Soviet Writers in 1934, played a significant role in East Germany during the late 1940s and early 1950s. It was the continuation of the anti-Formalist arguments from the 1930s by former Moscow-based émigrés such as Erpenbeck that helped cement the hegemony of Soviet cultural policy in this period. The features of *Mother Courage* criticised by Erpenbeck included the interruptive songs with their overt didacticism. Erpenbeck was not alone in his wariness of the didactic. Immediately after the war, many who had been bullied or seduced by Nazi propaganda turned their backs on any form of political pedagogy. This response partly explains the prevalent dismissive attitude, at least until late 1954, towards the *Proletkult*, a defamatory term for the revolutionary workers' art traditions during the Weimar Republic, especially agitprop forms and also Brecht's *Lehrstück*.

For the left-conservatives the only traditions that passed muster were nineteenth-century bourgeois realism and an approved group of German classics, starting with Lessing, Goethe and Schiller. These traditions, or so their proponents asserted, were more accessible and familiar to a broader cross section of the population and thus better able to offer reassurance to a traumatized population. The German classics were also lauded as examples of progressive humanism, a communal heritage that could help bring about the peaceful reunification of the divided nation. Uninterrupted illusionism was the usual representational mode of these traditions and it was one preferred by critics like Erpenbeck, who contended that what distinguished theatre from the classroom was its power to create an illusion of real social life happening in the here and now. Socialist Realist dramaturgy utilized many features of these traditions, adding covertly didactic features, such as the hero or heroine with whom the audience could identify and whose actions or virtues paved the way for a collective society. Rather than a unifying aesthetic of identification that helped conceal the theatre's didactic function, *Mother Courage* boldly asserted a counter-model that overtly challenged the bourgeois illusionist tradition and criticised the *petit bourgeois* aspirations that Hitler had appealed to so effectively (see Chapter 2). Such strategies were a risky business. The lead player in the SED, the First Secretary Walter Ulbricht, remained a staunch supporter of the classics and there were a number of occasions in the early 1950s when the Ensemble had reason to fear it would be dissolved as an independent theatre. Fortunately, events like the triumph in Paris ensured its longevity.

PEDAGOGUE OF PEACE AND RECONSTRUCTION

Brecht's output in the GDR, both his dissenting counter-models and his more orthodox work, was energized by his interpretation of the educational role art should play in the transition to socialism, and then stateless communism. In a country ravaged by fascism and war he believed it imperative that government and artists work together on re-education goals such as:

- exposing the origins and residue of Nazism and capitalist imperialism;
- enhancing public dialogue about socialism and its construction;
- celebrating the GDR's progress.

For Brecht the sobering events of June 1953 – the first workers' strike against a workers' state – confirmed the necessity of such a programme. In his eyes a significant causal factor behind the strike was the government's 'revolutionary haste'. In a bid to develop heavy industry as rapidly as possible, the government had made the error of imposing, without sufficient dialogue, a number of economic measures that proved detrimental to the workers' living standards. It had also failed to address the diverse background and ideology of the post-war workers who included former bourgeois Nazi Party members ousted from their posts in administration, as well as professional soldiers. The straw that broke the camel's back was the government's decision to raise the output required of industrial workers by 10 per cent. On 16 June miners took to the streets, demonstrating in front of the ministerial building in Berlin. The next day they returned, but this time their ranks were swelled with dissatisfied citizens calling for the end of the government and free elections. By the middle of the day Soviet tanks were rolling into the city centre.

Immediately prior to this military action Brecht had posted letters to three key political figures in which he declared his support for the government, enquired whether the Academy of Arts and Ensemble could be of assistance, and stressed the importance of dialogue with the masses about the tempo of socialist construction. Brecht then went to observe the demonstration first hand. His interpretation of the military defence, as a timely intervention against organized fascist elements intent on using the workers' dissatisfaction to topple the state and take Berlin to the brink of a third world war, was in line with the official SED position (Brecht 2003: 332). However, for him the street performance, with workers singing the *Internationale* (the anthem of international revolutionary socialism) being drowned out by the strength of those chanting 'Deutschland, Deutschland, über alles' (the first line from the banned national anthem, the singing of which was considered an extreme right-wing statement) also expressed the Party's failure thus far to empower the workers against Nazi ideology.

Brecht felt that de-Nazification could not be achieved by a cultural policy that exclusively highlighted the best of Germany's past, and thus he continued to create theatre that addressed problematic aspects of national history and their contemporary relevance. For example, in his 1950 adaptation of J.M.R. Lenz's 1771 tragicomedy, *The Tutor*, Brecht thematized the 'German *misère*', a label applied by left-wing commentators to highlight the repressive nature of the period that marked Germany's transition from a feudal to a bourgeois capitalist society. To Brecht's mind this painful epoch had been unnecessarily prolonged because of the acquiescence of the German bourgeoisie in the ideology of feudal society. Through a satirical depiction of a young tutor trapped in a servile relationship to the aristocracy of the late eighteenth century, he sought to offer a useful critique of the founding moments of the bourgeois education system at a time when educational reform was high on the GDR's agenda (Subiotto 1975: 15–16). Within the ranks of the Ensemble a similar reform was under way. Convinced that the GDR had inherited the Hitler Youth, 'educated to destroy the world, but not educated to live in a world that has been destroyed' (BBA 66/45 trans. Spiers 1982: 179), he had company members study Marxist-Leninist texts on a weekly basis. Brecht and Weigel's approach to casting also ensured that their young actors had access to experienced performers who had not absorbed the emotive charismatic style popular under Hitler's regime, including those who worked in leftist theatre during the Weimar Republic, former émigrés, and guests from the Zurich Schauspielhaus.

On the related subject of imperialist warfare, productions like Brecht's *Trumpets and Drums* (1955) supported the Party line against Western imperialism. An adaptation of George Farquhar's *The Recruiting Officer* (1706), Brecht's satirical play complemented the Party's criticism of recent Cold War developments. These included the remilitarization of West Germany and its mooted entry into the North Atlantic Treaty Organization (NATO), a military defence alliance of North American and European countries. But the staging of *Trumpets and Drums* also foregrounded the connection between imperialism and the ubiquitous socialization of men as colonizers, particularly in the army and law. In doing so it implicitly spoke against imperialist conditioning within any country. Through features such as the way the female drag role was staged – in order to be with her beloved Captain Plume, Victoria Balance dresses as Squire Wilful, enters the army, and successfully metamorphoses into the soldier Sergeant Wilful – the production demonstrated how militaristic masculinity was not innate so much as learned within a particular type of society (Mumford 1998: 247).

Moved by both his experience of two world wars and his dread of resurgent Nazism, Brecht maintained a vigilant stance against war mongering and territorialist machismo, both of which he associated with capitalism, a stance forcefully expressed in his poem 'To my Countrymen' (1948):

> You men, reach for the spade and not the knife.
> You'd sit in safety under roofs today
> Had you not used the knife to make your way
> And under roofs one leads a better life.
> I beg you, take the spade and not the knife.

(Brecht 1979c: 417)

In addition to anti-war plays, he prepared letters and declarations and spoke at congresses in support of Germany's peaceful reunification. In recognition of his contribution, he was awarded the International Stalin Peace Prize on 22 May 1955, an event met with consternation from many quarters on the other side of the border.

Brecht's satirical treatments of the 'German *misère*' and imperialism continued his long-established practice of estranging capitalist society. However, he acknowledged that socialist reconstruction also required a theatre that could inform its audience about the nature and achievements of revolutionary change. Through productions like *Katzgraben* (1953), Brecht sought to develop new practices that would meet this need. Erwin Strittmatter's Socialist Realist *Katzgraben* was the first and only contemporary East German play Brecht directed. Strittmatter was a farmer's son, and for Brecht the fact that the author had become a writer at all – and in Brecht's eyes a good one – was testimony to the success of the GDR's dismantling of the bourgeois monopoly on education. The text also addressed what he had consistently lauded in public and in private as the genuine achievements of the GDR, land reform after the expulsion of the Junker squires and schooling for proletarian youth (Philpotts 2003: 63–6). For instance, its **Fabel** – 'the plot of the play told as a sequence of interactions' (Weber, in Thomson and Sacks 1994: 181) – outlines the victory of small farmers against larger landowners. Their success results from a combination of individual enterprise, sympathetic leadership and help from the Party in the form of tractors and scientific education.

Having mastered the art of defamiliarizing the known, Brecht now experimented with familiarization strategies in order to give his city audience access to the 'foreign' world of rural life. These strategies included:

- an emphasis on detailed observation, exemplified in the documentary-style set and costumes based on a field trip to the village area where the play is set;
- individualistic characterization, to which end Strittmatter composed character *résumés* for the actors, with an emphasis on social background, and the production programme incorporated diary extracts and letters supposedly composed by the characters.

Brecht also encouraged actors to develop an empathetic relationship with their character wherever it served the social commentary of the

Fabel of *Katzgraben*. For example, concerned that Erwin Geschonneck's ridicule of the wealthy farmer Herr Grossmann actually undermined the farmer's credibility as a threatening opponent in the class struggle, Brecht urged the actor to subjectively justify his character by thinking of him as an intelligent man, only overturned by the new situation. An empathetic approach to a character's emotional state of being was also used to help introduce unfamiliar progressive elements such as the humanized socialist figure Steinert, miner and local Party Secretary. An antidote to the poker-faced stoic type of hero, what Brecht described as the ideal capitalist in disguise, Steinert presented a new male role model who did not conceal his feelings of uncertainty and helplessness. As Brecht put it, the 'human face under socialism must again be a mirror for feelings' (Brecht, in Mumford 1995: 254).

Katzgraben coincided with the peak both of Brecht's Stanislavsky studies and of the Stanislavsky wave in the GDR. At the First German Stanislavsky Conference in April 1953, only one month before the staging of *Katzgraben*, the Russian's methods were vigorously promoted as the best means to realize Socialist Realism. Brecht's engagement with Stanislavsky during *Katzgraben* was no doubt influenced by the pressure to conform to cultural policy. However, just as the choice of Strittmatter's play expressed a sustained commitment to social reform, the Stanislavsky studies reflected a genuine desire to equip a young company with the range of tools necessary both to defend and to constructively criticise such reform. Assisted by the publication flurry that accompanied the Stanislavsky wave, Brecht gained greater access to Stanislavsky's period of work after the Russian Revolution, particularly his everyday training and rehearsal practices. It was here in particular that he found approaches that could be readily modified to suit his materialist *Fabel*-oriented theatre:

- attention to contradictions and concrete historical detail;
- organization of crowd scenes;
- analytical segmentation of the action;
- attention to physical actions and the play's super-objective.

Whereas in the 1930s Brecht had rejected Stanislavsky's emphasis on empathetic relations with the character, he now adapted techniques like emotion memory and *résumés* to facilitate complex contradictory characterizations, and to create a dialectic between demonstration and experience (see Chapter 2). However, Brecht continued to view Stanislavsky's interpretive practice as non-Marxist, and to counter his emphasis on emotional truth with an insistence on critical demonstration informed by social truth.

While minute taking was not new at the Ensemble, the extensive nature of the rehearsal notes written by Brecht and his crew of assistants during *Katzgraben* testifies both to the influence of Stanislavsky and to the depth of Brecht's commitment. In addition to their important function as a means of recording performance, Brecht often used the documentation for pedagogical purposes. The existence of a bound volume of selected notes and photos from the staging suggests he was hoping to publish his practical experiments in an instructive format similar to the so-called *Modellbuch* ('model book'). A practice initiated by Berlau, each 'model book' contained a sequence of photos with captions, detailing significant gestures, positions, groupings and turning points in a particular production. One of their functions was to inform future theatre practitioners of Brecht's Marxist art of 'scenic writing' (Weber in Thomson and Sachs 1994: 181), a form of storytelling typified by socially significant **comportment**, *Arrangements* and tableaux. Brecht involved his cohort of young, contracted assistants in the production of these books, not only as a cost-cutting measure, but because he believed the task of selecting and glueing the production photos would improve their critical eye. The male assistants in particular were not enamoured of this teaching method, and found the collaborative work on rehearsals a more fruitful training ground. Here Brecht would seat himself in the stalls at a point where he could assess the choreography, and actively seek input and solutions from the collaborators, assistants and curious onlookers around him as well as the actors on stage (Figure 1.5). At last Brecht was able to rekindle the dialogic rehearsal practice he had so enjoyed prior to the exile years.

FOR THE PLEASURE OF THE RIVER-DWELLERS

Like a children's nursery on a sunny day, these rehearsals were usually characterized by an atmosphere of playful experimentation, humour and relaxation. Brecht had long insisted that the labour of art should be fun, but in the context of a new society that promised to remove exploitation and divisions between work and enjoyment, the issue of

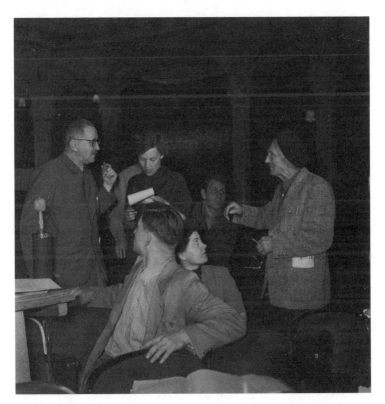

Figure 1.5 Brecht at a rehearsal of *The Caucasian Chalk Circle* with (from left) Isot Kilian, Hans Bunge, Käthe Rülicke, Manfred Wekwerth and actor Ernst Busch. Photo by Horst E. Schulze, © Bildarchiv Preußischer Kulturbesitz

pleasurable production acquired a new relevance. In his 'A Short Organum for the Theatre' (1948), an exposition designed to provide an up-do-date introduction to his theatre aesthetic and written prior to his first trip to the Soviet zone, Brecht called for the arts to 'recall that their task is to entertain the children of the scientific age, and to do so with sensuousness and humour'. To this end he advocated a theatre of pleasurable analysis, invention and intervention. A theatre that emancipated because its accurate 'representation of happenings between human beings' gave the pleasure of insight and an enjoyable experience of changing the world for the better (*BT* 204, 183). Here spectators had the opportunity both to witness the flow of life's river and to learn a productive critical attitude that could help them regulate it for the common good:

> Our representations of human social life are designed for river-dwellers, fruit farmers, builders of vehicles and upturners of society, whom we invite into our theatres and beg not to forget their cheerful occupations while we hand the world over to their minds and hearts, for them to change as they think fit.
>
> (*BT* 185)

Thanks to the resources put at Brecht's disposal in the GDR, he was able to realize the type of sensuous entertainment he advocated. Brecht also began to elaborate on his aesthetic of the naive, of producing pleasurably lucid and concentrated expressions of contradictory reality. The paintings of late medieval Flemish artist Pieter Brueghel – landscapes populated by peasants and rich with pictorial contrasts – and scientific expressions like physicist Isaac Newton's third law of motion – 'for each action there is an equal and opposite reaction' – exemplify the quality of intelligent simplicity that Brecht increasingly promoted. To enhance the GDR's experimental cultural playground he also applied himself to the development of German comedy and comedic performance, a reflection of his understanding that humour – in both its satirical and cheerful modes – was an important emancipatory force.

Equipped with his own apparatus and in the midst of a society aiming to achieve social production – by and for the people rather than for private profit – Brecht experienced the most intense period of collective creativity in his life. Unfortunately his health did not keep pace with his enthusiasm for productive assent and dissent, be it in the form of staging, adaptation, teaching, theorizing, cultural policy or poetry. Due to his deteriorating health, a new production of *Galileo* had to be postponed. He was never to see the final version. On 14 August 1956, after a prolonged struggle with a heart condition, Brecht died of a coronary thrombosis. In accordance with his wishes, he was buried in the Dorotheen Cemetery neighbouring his Berlin apartment. Here Brecht's grave joined that of G.W.F. Hegel, the early nineteenth-century idealist whose dialectical philosophy Marx had challenged and reworked for his materialist agenda. In this staging of the graveyard scene, Brecht once again proved himself a man who took great pleasure in the wit of contradiction and 'the possibilities of change in all things' (*BT* 202).

BRECHT TODAY?

In light of the momentous political and environmental changes that have taken place since Brecht's death it has become more difficult to share his optimistic vision of progress towards a world beyond exploitation and class division. The Cold War has abated, but the victor has been global capitalism rather than international communism. Germany has been reunified, but little remains of the socialist republic. Scientific technology has greatly increased our productive capacities, but it has exacerbated rather than resolved world poverty. In such a context, Brecht's diagnosis of the ills of capitalist society, including its misuse of science, continues to resonate. But his odes to progressive river-dwellers, tractors and scientific education can seem quaint and dusty. What, then, does Brecht offer contemporary artists and teacher-learners interested in representing, or even changing, society? This book responds to that question by exploring his revolutionary methods for challenging the way we create and imagine the social world and ourselves. While Brecht's Marxist narrative is in need of revision, he can still help us to know the interpretive frameworks within which we operate, to transform our oppressive positions, and to develop what it takes to master the complex art of pleasurable production.

2

BRECHT'S KEY THEORIES

BRECHT IN DIALOGUE

Brecht was an extraordinary writer. He was prolific, collaborative, openly partisan and seriously playful. Just a glance at the most recent edition of his writings gives a good sense of the scope of Brecht's range. Comprising thirty volumes in total, the *Berliner und Frankfurter* edition includes more than forty theatre plays as well as screenplays, adaptations, poems, a novel, stories, letters, diary and work journal entries. This incredible output testifies to the intense nature of Brecht's interest in both writing and productivity. Significantly, almost one fifth of this work consists of theoretical commentary on art and politics, in particular the politics of theatre. This chapter will focus on key texts and ideas in this commentary, eloquent testimony to the importance Brecht attributed to critical reflection on both art and society.

Brecht's commentaries celebrate his belief that thought is a product of social interaction and the problem-solving energy of collaboration. He makes the social nature of thought explicit through obvious references – sometimes reverential, sometimes parodic – to writers and texts that have greatly influenced his work and culture. For example, Brecht's famous use of the term 'epic' to describe his plays and theatre draws upon and challenges the influential thought of the ancient Greek philosopher Aristotle who, in *Poetics*, a treatise on literary theory, ranks the dramatic genre of tragedy above the epic. Brecht's frequent use of dialogue conveys his interest in the age-old practice of collaborative thinking. Take, for instance, the unfinished project known to us as *The Messingkauf Dialogues* (1939–55), an attempt to bring together the fruits of his earlier theoretical texts into an ordered whole. In it a number of characters – such as The Actor, The Dramaturg, The Stagehand, The Philosopher – pose questions and dialogue about their respective approaches to theatre practice. The *Modellbücher* ('model books') created by Brecht and his colleagues, each a collection of photos and explanatory notes from his post-1945 productions, demonstrate a similar desire to test theatre theory through dialogue. The unfinished *Katzgraben* model book (c. 1953) incorporates edited versions of actual conversations – theoretical reflections, in effect – between people involved in the production – Brecht, his directorial assistants, his scenographer and Strittmatter, the playwright – which establish the ideas and principles upon which Brecht's socialist theatre making is founded. These conversations are also a very valuable insight into one of the ways in which Brecht pursued a dialogue between theoretical commentary, playwriting and staging.

THEORY IN DIALOGUE WITH OTHER CREATIVE PRACTICES

During the *Katzgraben* rehearsals in 1953, Brecht noted that his theorizing sprang from an inability to resist sharing his technique and ideas, as well a desire to ensure the efficacy of his work:

> … my plays have to be properly performed if they are to be effective, so that for the sake of (oh dear me!) a non-**aristotelian** dramaturgy I had to outline (calamity!) an **epic theatre**.

(*BT* 248)

But is John Fuegi correct when he argues that, while for Brecht theory had a valuable place outside the theatre, it had almost no place in his day-by-day staging practice (Fuegi 1987: xiii)? In order to address this issue it is important to clarify what exactly is meant by 'theory' and 'practice'. Throughout this book 'practice' is defined as the action of doing something, so theorizing – i.e. thinking or writing about ideas and principles of practice – is *a part of*, inseparable from, practice, and not *apart from*, in opposition to, it. While it is true that theory involves a much greater degree of written or verbal *observation and analysis of* activities, it does share common ground with other forms of language-based creative practices. Accordingly, I shall define 'theory' as a contemplative linguistic practice.

In his later years as director at the Berliner Ensemble, his first chance to engage extensively in production work, Brecht took a careful approach towards the role of theoretical commentary during the process of staging. For instance, he did not spend much rehearsal time discussing ideas and jargon, preferring to concentrate on experimentation with action and **Arrangement**. Nevertheless, he did draw on characteristic 'Brechtian' terminology and his co-workers certainly used words like '**Gestus**' and '**Verfremdung**' in their rehearsal notes. Brecht's attitude towards theory at this point was shaped not only by the immediate political situation in the German Democratic Republic (GDR), but also by his long-held enthusiasm for Marx's early promotion of interventionist thinking.

During the early 1950s Brecht was targeted by the cultural critics of the young GDR who vigorously promoted Soviet **Socialist Realism** (see the section on realism on page 87) and Stanislavsky's model of realist theatre. Brecht had to defend himself against accusations that he was a Formalist, an artist obsessed with form at the expense of social content. According to Brecht these accusations stemmed from a misuse of his theoretical writings. For example, he detected a tendency on the part of critics to transform his theory and other creative practices into something unnecessarily complicated and removed from everyday social existence, when they were actually derived from naive observations of people's behaviour and opinions as well as a deep concern with the art of living. He also criticised the erroneous assumption that his theory was some sort of comprehensive and total entity, the last word, when of course it was full of silences. As he noted in 1953, while an 'enormous quantity' of *old* rules of performance were preserved in the production work at the Berliner Ensemble, their usefulness was rarely addressed in the theoretical writings (*BT* 248).

Brecht's approach to theory was also guided by one of Marx's early theses from 1845: 'The philosophers have only interpreted the world in various ways; the point is, to change it' (Marx 1977: 390). The material practice of observing and contemplating should be integrated with the practice of revolutionary political action. Through that integration, theory itself will be transformed by social reality. At the Ensemble, Brecht neither divorced theory from staging nor allowed it to dominate. Instead, he sought to embody and correct theory through the improvised social actions of the performers – their play with gestures, attitudes and positioning. Brecht tested the efficacy of his playscripts in the same way, showing surprise at his own writing and changing his texts willingly mid-rehearsal when something the actors did illuminated a problem or threw up a better solution. Theory was again revised in the light of audience response. As Brecht often put it, the proof of the pudding lies in the eating. Brecht's fondness for this proverb is sometimes interpreted as proof that he was more than willing to sacrifice dry epic theories for the sake of great art and cathartic entertainment. Well, Brecht certainly aimed to provide quality entertainment, but for him the measuring rod was not catharsis but whether a way of *looking at* and *acting within* the world had been challenged. And to this end, an ongoing dialogue between theorizing, staging and public performance was crucial. We can get a fuller sense of the richness of Brecht's approach to this naive saying when we compare it with the way the proverb was used by Engels and Brecht's unorthodox Marxist mentor, Karl Korsch. Like these theorists, Brecht employed the proverb to endorse the pragmatic view that we can test and correct our sense-perception of objects and qualities (the pudding or epic drama and theatre) by putting the objects to use (by eating or staging). Did the spectator have a revolutionary, life-altering meal? Or was a different mixture of ingredients and methods required in order to create the pudding that would change the culinary habits of a lifetime?

THEORY MEETS POETRY IN MOTION

There is another reason why Brecht's theoretical writings should not be divorced from his other creative practices. Like the poetry and playscripts, many of his commentaries on art and politics are playful. Yes, there are terse and even tedious passages, but look out too for the following sorts of games: the mischievous use of irony and paradox, the 'tongue-in-cheek' tone, the switches between different speaking voices (as in the scripted dialogues), the fun with polysemes (words with many meanings) and the use of old terms in new ways (words like '*Gestus*' and 'epic', for example). When you do not read German, it is sometimes hard to get a sense of how playful Brecht's commentaries can be, simply because the translator is often compelled to put conceptual accuracy first. Fortunately, the scholarly translations now available in English manage to provide an authentic taste of his commentary puddings. Their editorial notes also remind us that these writings were poetry-in-motion; never a monolithic doctrine, fixed and coherent, but sketches on the move, unfinished and at times contradictory. This is not simply because they were often written in haste, as their author hopped from one project, country and political situation to another over a period of almost forty years, but because Brecht consciously sought to engage an ever-changing reality in new-minted dialogue.

BRECHT'S KEY CONCERNS

Despite the fact that Brecht was a prolific philosopher-poet for whom 'change' was a watchword, there were issues relating to the craft and politics of theatre that – especially after his engagement with Marxism in 1926 – he continually returned to, even if he modified his position at each visit. In this chapter, these issues are explored through a discussion of the following topic areas:

- *Gestus*
- *Verfremdung* (**defamiliarization**)
- **historicization**
- epic theatre
- **dialectics**
- realism

The chapter also contains a brief analysis of three key texts that span the decade from 1930 to 1940, a period when Brecht wrote far more essays of substantial length on aesthetics and politics that at any other time in his career (see Brecht 2003: 3). These texts provide helpful starting points for understanding the chosen topic areas. All three are available in *Brecht on Theatre: The Development of an Aesthetic* (1964), or *BT* as it is referred to in this book, a volume of Brecht's writings edited and translated by John Willett:

1 'On Gestic Music', 1937;
2 'Short Description of a New Technique of Acting which Produces a Defamiliarization Effect', c. 1940 (I have translated *Verfremdung* as 'defamiliarization', *not*, as Willett does, **'alienation'**);
3 'Notes to the Opera *The Rise and Fall of the City of Mahagonny*', 1930 (this is the article's final title. Willett uses a sentence from the article – 'The modern theatre is the epic theatre' – as the main title).

In keeping with Brecht's own interweaving of contemplative and creative practice, each topic area discussed in this chapter combines discussion of his theories with examples of staging taken from his Berliner Ensemble productions (1949–56).

GETTING THE GIST OF *GESTUS*

If there is one term in Brecht's theorizing that best illustrates his passion for wordplay and a dialogue between politics and art, then it is the polyseme *Gestus*. The term is pronounced 'Guest-oos', but English-language readers who find themselves frustrated by its many meanings are advised to seek relief by pronouncing it 'Jest-us'! While Brecht and his co-workers at the Berliner Ensemble tended to use theoretical jargon sparingly during rehearsals, the frequent occurrence of *Gestus* is a notable exception. This is partly because in German the Latin word is interchangeable with *Geste* ('gesture') and *Gestik* ('gesticulation'). Sometimes Brecht used *Gestus* simply to mean 'gesture' in the sense of a purely physical expression. Sometimes he used it in the sense of 'gesticulation' to refer to a complex of different types of gesture, including verbalizations. However, from the late 1920s onwards he became increasingly interested in gesture as socially encoded expression. Socialized gesture includes movement that is consciously employed, such as a nod or shake of the head. It also refers to the moulded and sometimes subconscious body language of a person from a particular social **class** or workplace, such as the genteel manners of a group of diplomats as they stir their tea or the posture of a farmer just back from a day's labour in the fields, who converses with tired hands resting on his knees. Brecht's theatre work at the Ensemble placed a new emphasis on such gesticulation, especially that connected with habits, manners and customs. For example, he would pay particular attention to the taking of a bow or the doffing of a hat. This emphasis was inspired by performers like Charlie Chaplin, who as early as 1914 (Brecht first saw a Chaplin film in 1921) was already making his body express socialized behaviour in a way that interested Brecht. From the 1930s onwards, Brecht's assertion of a gestic (= *Gestus* and gesture-oriented) theatre was also fuelled by his antipathy towards psychological theatre, which he accused of focusing on facial expression, 'the mirror of the soul', to the point where other gesticulation 'dried up' (Brecht 1965: 28).

After coming into contact with Marxism, Brecht began to play with a further two Latin meanings of the term '*Gestus*'. The word can denote the gestures made by actors or orators according to the rules of art in order to give additional physical expressiveness to their words. This notion of artistically crafted and persuasive gestures fitted Brecht's theatre of partisan demonstration very nicely. Of even greater usefulness was the Latin use of the term to mean 'bearing', 'carriage', 'posture' and 'attitude'. In this chapter these meanings are all expressed under the portmanteau word **'comportment'** – *the socially conditioned relation to time, space and people of a thinking body*. The German word that usually covers these meanings is '*Haltung*', and it invariably popped up when Brecht was talking about *Gestus*. Increasingly Brecht brought the two Latin meanings together to define *Gestus* as the artistic selection and demonstration of comportment. To cut a long word game short, we find Brecht using *Gestus* in a rather slippery way throughout his writings to mean one or all of the following: social (ized) gesticulation as opposed to psychological facial expression; contextualized and alterable comportment; and the rhetorical crafted gestures of a performer. From the late 1920s Brecht repeatedly combined these meanings, contriving a rich amalgam of ideas that formed the core of his political theatre. To 'show the *Gestus*' came to mean *to present artistically the mutable socio-economic and ideological construction of human behaviour and relations.*

In order to unpack the various implications of this abstract definition, it is worth discussing a more digestible version as well as some concrete examples from Brecht's Ensemble work. A good starting point is John Willett's definition from *The Theatre of Bertolt Brecht*:

> It [*Gestus*] is at once gesture and gist, attitude and point: one aspect of the relation between two people, studied singly, cut to essentials and physically or

verbally expressed. It excludes the psychological, the subconscious, the metaphysical, unless they can be conveyed in concrete terms.

(Willett 1977: 173)

The phrase 'at once gesture and gist' is a timely reminder that at the
heart of both *Gestus* and Brecht's theatre is the interweaving of sensual
activities (gestures) and ideas or social meanings (gists). Willett's
definition also acknowledges the artistic nature of *Gestus*, his 'cut to
essentials' implying a selection and shaping process. However, his
association of *Gestus* with 'attitude' is only helpful if we rid ourselves
of the tendency to see 'attitude' as meaning simply an individual's
mental response, or, worse, a given psychological disposition. Rather,
in Brecht's theatre, attitude is both a socially conditioned mental
stance *and* body orientation in space and time. Brecht was not interested in psychological or metaphysical drama that presented the
mental attitudes of its protagonists as the product of innate, God-
given or unknowable forces. Nor did he wish to depict attitudes born
of irreversible conditions such as mental and terminal illness. Rather,
he wanted to open up for scrutiny behaviour that had been learned,
that was liable to change. This is why, for example, in the Ensemble
production of *Mother Courage and Her Children* he drew attention to
the comportment of peasants who resort to the ineffectual custom of
kneeling and praying whenever their lives are in danger. Brecht's gestic
theatre asks: why and to what end do people comport themselves as
they do? Can and should their social bearing or stance be changed?

'ON GESTIC MUSIC'

Written in 1937 while Brecht was in Denmark in exile from the
Nazis, 'On Gestic Music' is the most detailed commentary on *Gestus*
available in English. Here Willett translates *Gestus* as 'gest' (using
'gests' as the plural). He also translates the German word *Haltung* as
'attitude', though it is worth keeping in mind that it can also mean
'bearing' and 'stance'. In the opening paragraph Brecht makes clear
that gestic art, including literature and music, must effectively convey

particular attitudes adopted by the speaker towards other men. The sentence
'pluck the eye that offends thee out' is less effective from the gestic point of
view than 'if thine eye offend thee, pluck it out'. The latter starts by presenting

the eye, and the first clause has the definite gest of making an assumption; the main clause then comes as a surprise, a piece of advice, and a relief.

(BT 104)

So, is *Gestus* just a new word for an old idea, i.e. the rhetorically effective expression of attitude? What is absent from Brecht's introduction – and from Willett's pithy definition – is any mention of the vital role played by his Marxist view of human relations. But be patient and you will find that Brecht starts to address this issue midway through his text:

Not all gests are social gests. The attitude of chasing away a fly is not yet a social gest, though the attitude of chasing away a dog may be one, for instance if it comes to represent a badly dressed man's continual battle against watchdogs. One's efforts to keep one's balance on a slippery surface result in a social gest as soon as falling down would mean 'losing face'; in other words, losing one's market value. The gest of working is definitely a social gest, because all human activity directed towards the mastery of nature is a social undertaking, an undertaking between men. On the other hand a gest of pain, as long as it is kept so abstract and generalized that it does not rise above a purely animal category, is not yet a social one …. The 'look of a hunted animal' can become a social gest if it is shown that particular manoeuvres by men can degrade the individual man to the level of a beast; the social gest is the gest relevant to society, the gest that allows conclusions to be drawn about the social circumstances.

(BT 104–5)

The distinction between 'gests' and 'social gests' is an attempt on Brecht's part (and the translator's, in one case) to clarify that his theatre does much more than simply present gesticulation and attitudes. Instead, it chooses *significant* gestures and then shows us how they are the result of particular social and historical forces rather than being eternal universal occurrences. By 'significant' Brecht means humans and events, which are most decisive for the developmental processes of society. Take, for example, the actions and comportment of an unemployed man during the Great Depression trying yet again to drive off a pack of dogs that are protecting a property he must rob if his family are to survive. These gestures are 'significant' because they tell us something about (dehumanizing) power relations and social structures that can be changed. Brecht's gestic theatre aims to present all gestures and contexts as social and 'man made' rather than as the mysterious hand of fate.

There are two concrete examples in 'On Gestic Music' that are brilliantly worked through in the Berliner Ensemble's 1950 production of *The Tutor*. The first is 'the attitude of chasing away a fly' and the second the *Gestus* of 'losing face' and market value after falling on a slippery surface. *The Tutor* is Brecht's adaptation of Jakob Michael Reinhold Lenz's *The Tutor: or The Advantages of Private Education* (1774). In Lenz's play the protagonist, Läuffer, is a young teacher who, unable to get work in the new municipal schools, has to take up a post as private tutor to Gustchen and Leopold, the children of Major von Berg, a country squire. After a degrading interview conducted by Major von Berg's wife, with Leopold and Count Wermuth looking on, Läuffer is accepted, but finds himself paid less than his agreed wage each year and denied social life both within the household and outside the town of Heidelbrunn. His sexual desires and isolation drive him into an affair with Gustchen, who in turn has been cut off from her beloved cousin Fritz. When Gustchen becomes pregnant, Läuffer flees, and is taken under the wing of a village schoolmaster. Out of remorse and despair he castrates himself. In Brecht's version Läuffer mutilates himself *out of fear for the social and career implications of his sexual feelings for the schoolmaster's ward, Lise.* Such changes, at a time when the GDR was reforming its education system, helped Brecht turn Lenz's text into a commentary on the behaviour of German intellectuals. In particular, his adaptation criticised their emasculating habit of 'bowing down' to the ruling class and serving a system they should oppose, both during the transition from feudal to capitalist society in the late eighteenth century, and under the Nazis. To this end, Brecht spent considerable time with the lead actor creating a gestic motif out of a series of 'unmanly' bows towards class superiors. The presentation of contradictory comportments during the bows – obsequiousness vs contempt, observing feudal etiquette vs overplaying it with rebellious vitality – suggested the transformability of Läuffer's inferior status: he need not be and remain subservient.

In the Ensemble staging of the interview scene, Brecht instructed the young actor playing Leopold to create a comic and telling *Gestus* out of the business of 'chasing away a fly'. According to Brecht's notes, as Läuffer clumsily attempts to prove he can dance a minuet, sweating and squirming under the watchful eye of the Major's wife at the spinet, 'Leopold, for the sake of whose education Läuffer is applying, is catching flies on the wall. He has seen a lot of such auditions' (BBA 547/01). Bryant-Bertail interprets the *Gestus* of fly-catching as a little act of resistance on the son's part: 'Leopold threw off the *misery of his education* for the moment, and, following the fly, managed to write a path of escape for himself and the spectators' (Bryant-Bertail 2000: 101). But perhaps there is more to this *Gestus*, especially if the fly is seen as a metaphor for Läuffer in the hands of the ruling class. The second example, the *Gestus* of 'losing face', Brecht recast as an elaborate pantomime scene – not in Lenz's original – in which Laüffer takes Leopold to the outdoor skating rink in the village and tries to gain the attention of the village girls by showing off on the ice (Figure 2.1). As he attempts to strike up a conversation he collides dramatically with Leopold. His fall creates a loss of market value *because it damages his prospects of marriage with a girl of his own class*. These two examples, plus Läuffer's bow, demonstrate that a *Gestus* cannot be achieved through a single gesture from a lone actor in isolation, but is

Figure 2.1 Läuffer just before he 'loses face' on the ice in the Berliner Ensemble production of *The Tutor*, 1950. Photo by Wolfgang Meyenfels, image courtesy of BBA

dependent upon the relationship between this gesture and the social context developed throughout the performance.

THE *GESTUS* OF SHOWING

These examples demonstrate that in both theory and practice *Gestus* refers to vivid gestural expression of social bearing and the social relationships prevailing among people at a given historical moment. For the actor, such gestural expression arises out of a Marxist, or politically interventionist, interpretation of a line, a character's basic attitude, a relationship. Brecht's Ensemble rehearsals for *The Tutor* also clarify how gestic theatre involves an approach to facial expression that is quite distinct from that of psychological theatre, as well as placing considerable emphasis on the *Gestus* of showing. One feature of the rehearsal discussion of facial expression was the focus on a person's gaze as a reflection of their class-based social bearing towards others, rather than as an externalization of spontaneous thoughts and feelings. For example, gaze was used to delineate the social position and attitude of both Count Wermuth and the Maid who ushers him into the room where Major von Berg's wife is interviewing Läuffer. After announcing the Count's arrival in an impassioned tone, the actress playing the Maid was to *show* her character's inability to remove her eyes from this elegant phenomenon (Figure 2.2). Her gaze was one of several gestures designed to demonstrate that the Maid's behaviour was illustrative of a 'significant' passive response of the working class: her blind admiration for the aristocratic elite reflected a devoted rather than rebellious attitude (BBA 1566/6). Her eyes reflected not the soul of a given psyche, but habit born of a combination of social conditioning and individual choice.

Brecht's work with the actress playing the Maid is in accordance with his appeal to the actor in 1945 to 'Show that you show!' Of all the artistic comportments in Brecht's theatre, the one he regarded as the most fundamental for the actor was the famous *Gestus* of showing. The act of 'showing that you are showing' is a feature of many presentational performances, including the popular entertainment and Asian traditions so admired by Brecht, as well as certain types of everyday performance. Brecht often cited fairground ballad singers, acrobats, Chinese actors, comedic performers as well as law-court witnesses as sources of inspiration for his 'theatre of demonstration'.

Figure 2.2 Gestus of devotion: the Maid gazes admiringly at Count Wermuth. Image courtesy of BBA

However, what is unique about the Brechtian actor is that he does not merely demonstrate subject matter or character, but *does so from the point of view of a socialist commentator* – a feature 'On Gestic Music' emphasizes by insisting that a composer's attitude to the text reflect his attitude to the class struggle.

VERFREMDUNG AND V-EFFECTS

The *Gestus* of showing is one of the main *Verfremdung* devices (or V-effects) Brecht used in order to encourage all theatre players to become socially critical observers. Like '*Gestus*', the term '*Verfremdung*' is the result of Brecht's playing with old words. '*Verfremdung*' (pronounced 'fair-frem-doong') first appeared in his writings in 1936, since when translators have had almost as much fun with it as Brecht did. 'Alienation' is the most common – and most unhelpful – translation, but there have been many others, including: 'de-alienation', 'disillusion', 'dislocation', 'distanciation' and 'estrangement'. All of these versions say something about the word and the artistic strategy it refers to. However, I prefer to use 'defamiliarization' because I think it conveys more clearly the fact that Brecht regarded *Verfremdung* as political intervention into the (blindingly) familiar.

In the 'Short Organum for the Theatre' Brecht cogently describes his V-effects as 'designed to free socially-conditioned phenomena from that stamp of familiarity which protects them against our grasp today' by means of a representation 'which allows us to recognize its subject, but at the same time makes it seem unfamiliar' (*BT* 192). Today, the Brechtian V-effect lives on in forms like the caricature sketches of politicians found in left-wing newspapers. On occasion, Brecht used *Verfremdung* to describe the strategies of various artists down the ages who have sought to arouse new, or revitalize old, perceptions through a process of 'making strange'. However, Brecht remained critical of those V-effects which supported conservative politics, turned objects into something incomprehensibly bizarre, or lacked social usefulness. It is his insistence that art should reveal 'society's causal network' (*BT* 109) which distinguishes his theory and practice of defamiliarization.

One source of inspiration for *Verfremdung* was the *jingu* (Chinese opera) actor Mei Lanfang, whom Brecht saw give an impromptu performance of a female role during a visit to Moscow in 1935. In a man's dinner jacket and without special lighting, Mei appeared to show, rather than conceal, his own demonstrational skills, not to 'become' his female character, but rather to 'quote' her. Mei's performance could well have been in Brecht's mind when, in around 1939–41, he had his *Messingkauf* Philosopher muse on the point of such cross-gender playing (Brecht 1965: 76–7). It might, he argued – like the cross-generational and cross-class casting also referred to in the same dialogue – help emphasize the way in which behaviour is socially constructed. It seems that Brecht never realized that in *jingu* the actor actually maintains an interior process of empathizing with his character (Martin 2000: 229), because he repeatedly presented Chinese acting as distinguished by a marked split between actor and character. Such a split, he argued, was ripe for transferral to a Marxist theatre of *Verfremdung*, one that asked of the actor that she both maintain critical distance from the character and reveal her (normally concealed) creative labour.

The centrality of *Verfremdung* to Brecht's political aesthetic is also due to its relationship with Marx's ideas about *Entfremdung* ('alienation'). According to Marx, humans alienate themselves from the products of their intellectual, economic and social activity when they forfeit control and ownership of a part of themselves (the self being a fluid combination of historically created possibilities) by making that part into an alien Other. Drawing on the thought of the philosopher Feuerbach (1804–72), Marx argues that religious alienation occurs when we create God, an imagined and supposedly higher being that is actually constructed from estranged aspects of our own self. Marx identified many forms of alienation, but it was to the economic alienation of the labourer in the capitalist system of commodity exchange that he devoted particular attention. Under **capitalism**, the labourer produces objects and services, including the machinery used by his fellow workers, that do not belong to him and which perpetuate an exploitative system that impoverishes him. Marx's revolutionary agenda was powered by his desire to combat humankind's forfeiture of control by promoting the creation of a classless society free from capitalist exploitation. Given Brecht's familiarity with the significance of *Entfremdung* for Marx, and his own vision of humans as capable of controlling their destiny, it is misleading to translate *Verfremdung* as 'alienation' (Mumford 2003: 1405). Far from wishing to plunge spectators into a state of alienation, Brecht sought to challenge a condition of alienation through a theatre of empowering observation.

A COLD SCIENTIFIC PRACTICE?

As a method of intervention, *Verfremdung* also bears the traces of Brecht's interest in the rational behaviour of scientists in fields such as the natural and social sciences as well as the arts and humanities. When he described the inquisitive attitude necessary to achieve defamiliarization, Brecht often referred to the way the scientist Galileo (1564–1642) turned the familiar motion of a swinging chandelier into something strange by observing it with astonishment. In turn, this state of excited detachment makes the phenomenon more comprehensible and controllable, just as Galileo's amazement at the pendulum motion allegedly enabled him to discover the laws by which it is governed. But can rational analysis properly be applied to an art form? Does not *Verfremdung* belong in the classroom or laboratory rather than the theatre? It is a popular misconception that *Verfremdung* leads to non-emotional, even tedious theatre, despite the fact that, as Brecht himself explained, scientists experience great emotional excitement, shock and wonder while observing and discovering something about phenomena. For Brecht, thinking and feeling were inextricably linked, and the process of learning immense fun and hugely emotional. Moreover, he wanted a theatre that combined the emotions of scientific process with those of passionate partisanship. Not only wonderment and discovery, but emotions Brecht regarded as socially productive – like anger and irritation at injustice – were a vital component of a political theatre keen to nurture problem-solving activists.

One reason for the common misunderstanding that defamiliarization is a cold, emotion-free zone is Brecht's early polemical rejection of certain forms of **empathy** and identification. Brecht remained suspicious of the tendency in **dramatic theatre** to use these processes to channel the energy of both actors and spectators towards having *similar* emotions to the *character*. In his view it reinforced the tendency to believe these experiences familiar, real and normal rather than to ask whether they are the norm and, if so, whether they should be. His wariness was greatly heightened by Hitler's hypnotic theatre, in which the German public were encouraged to see the world only through the Führer's eyes. Nor did Brecht have any time for what he called 'Fascism's grotesque emphasizing of the emotions' and its 'threat to the rational element in Marxist aesthetics' (*BT* 145). Instead he wanted to safeguard against 'unduly impulsive, frictionless and uncritical creation of characters and incidents' (*BT* 137) and to stop audiences from leaving their critical faculties in the cloakroom, along with their hats.

Initially, Brecht's concern about the passive responses he felt were induced by empathy led him to demand that it be minimized in a theatre of *Verfremdung*. However, in his 1954 appendices to the 'Short Organum', he shows a greater awareness of the way his theatre always thrived on a complex interplay between referring to the familiar (with the help of empathic understanding) and making the familiar strange (through critical demonstration):

> The contradiction between acting (demonstration) and experience (empathy) often leads the uninstructed to suppose that only one or the other can be manifest in the work of the actor …. In reality it is naturally a matter of two mutually [antagonistic] processes which fuse in the actor's work; … His particular effectiveness comes from the tussle and tension of the two opposites, and also from their depth.
>
> (*BT* 277–8)

Brecht also became more attuned to how the use of empathy and demonstration was (and should be) guided by sensitivity to current historical and social circumstances. During rehearsals for the Ensemble's *Katzgraben*, a contemporary East German play by Erwin Strittmatter, Brecht found empathy to be a valuable tool for helping his city audience to engage with the play's presentation of agricultural heroes and reform. Until he moved to the GDR in 1949, Brecht had devoted himself largely to defamiliarizing bourgeois capitalist behaviour, often through negative examples. However, in the young communist country he now needed to find a way of making the new heroes and practices familiar at the same time as defamiliarizing the old habits that die hard (Mumford 1995: 252–4).

One of Brecht's most memorable criticisms of a theatre based on arousing total empathy with character can be found in his essay 'Theatre for Pleasure or Theatre for Instruction' (1935):

> The dramatic theatre's spectator says: Yes, I have felt like that too – Just like me – It's only natural – It'll never change – The sufferings of this man appal me, because they are inescapable – That's great art; it all seems the most obvious thing in the world – I weep when they weep, I laugh when they laugh.

> The epic theatre's spectator says: I'd never have thought it – That's not the way – That's extraordinary, hardly believable – It's got to stop – The sufferings of this man appal me, because they are unnecessary – That's great art: nothing obvious in it – I laugh when they weep, I weep when they laugh.

> *(BT 71)*

Brecht's spectator continues to laugh and cry but, as this makes clear, his reasons differ markedly from those of the 'dramatic' spectator. Rather than being moved by what is presented as the familiar and inescapable, she is outraged by the unnecessary. Rather than simply repeating the character's emotions, epic theatre aims to create tensions between an array of emotions. What this commentary fails to clarify is the way the experience of emotions and attitudes analogous to the character's continues to play a role in epic theatre. This is because Brecht wanted both actor and spectator to have an informed or engaged understanding of many points of view, *including that of the character*. However, because Brecht presented the questioning actor as a model for the spectator to identify with, he shifted the focus from empathy *with the character* to a novel emphasis on empathy *with the socially critical actor*. In those moments when the epic spectator and actor have an emotional response that is diametrically opposed to that of the character, the conflict adds a further layer of emotional intensity. Far from removing emotion, *Verfremdung* sets in motion a complex friction that can generate considerable emotional heat.

'SHORT DESCRIPTION OF A NEW TECHNIQUE OF ACTING WHICH PRODUCES A DEFAMILIARIZATION EFFECT' (1940)

Brecht's most comprehensive essay on the application of *Verfremdung* is his 'Short Description of a New Technique of Acting which Produces a Defamiliarization Effect', written when he was in exile from the Nazis and helping his actress wife, Helene Weigel, with her teaching work in a Swedish acting school. As well as showing the inter-connected nature of *Verfremdung* and the other key elements in Brecht's theatre, it contains many concrete examples of how theatre makers can create V-effects. The following discussion of the essay will cite references to ways in which actors have created (or failed to create) V-effects in productions, especially Brecht's, of *Mother Courage and Her Children*. His actors' work demonstrates vividly that *Verfremdung* is not about decoratively grafting artistic devices mentioned in essays like 'Short Description' onto a production. Rather, it is a matter of employing these devices in accordance with an inter-ventionist interpretation.

Many of the V-effects discussed early on in 'Short Description' are anti-illusionist, contrived to disrupt the illusion that what is occurring on stage is real life unfolding spontaneously before our eyes. In the realist theatre of Stanislavsky and others, that was dominant in Brecht's day and still predominates in mainstream Western theatre today, this illusion is conjured from a bag of tricks, such as:

- a darkened auditorium and atmospheric lighting that makes the audience lose awareness of their neighbours and become involved in the stage events and characters instead;
- concealed audio-visual sources, such as hidden light sources and musicians, and a stage curtain drawn to hide set changes;
- historically authentic props, sets and costumes;

- the erection of an invisible 'fourth wall' between stage and audi-torium to enable a mode of performance in which the actor behaves *as if* he is the character and *as if* the audience are not present.

Brecht used *Verfremdung* to expose this 'fourth-wall' illusionism as a tool for preserving the bourgeois status quo, arguing that manip-ulating spectators into close identification with characters and an involvement in an uninterrupted linear flow of action led to fatal-istic self-indulgence, in which any ability to reflect critically on social reality was inhibited. 'Short Description' contains a range of V-effects – visible technology, brilliant lighting, and direct address to the audience – which Brecht believed might expose the efforts of traditional theatre to hide and hypnotize. Elsewhere he refers to the famous half-height curtains that, through their partial revelation of set changes, signal that theatre is a human construct and the product of labour. The light linen curtains, strung on visible steel wires and often used as a projection space for anti-illusionist scene captions, allude mischievously to the illusionistic theatre's plush velvet curtain that veils the ability of humans to (re)construct their environment. Unfortunately, many of these devices have become hollow clichés in commercial theatres, where they are invariably disconnected from Brecht's socialist project and reduced to a marketable style.

'Short Description' also provides examples of rehearsal methods for defamiliarizing a character's behaviour. The actor is instructed to begin the characterization process by reading the part attentively – Brecht assumes a text-based theatre – with the attitude of 'a man who is astounded and contradicts' (*BT* 137). Anything that the actor finds unexpected about the character, or that she finds herself in opposition to, should be remembered and incorporated into the performance by a procedure Brecht calls 'fixing the not-but':

> [B]esides what he actually is doing he will at all essential points discover, specify, imply what he is not doing; that is to say he will act in such a way that the alternative emerges as clearly as possible, that his acting allows the other possibilities to be inferred and only represents one out of the possi-ble variants. He will say for instance 'You'll pay for that', and not say 'I forgive you'. He detests his children; it is not the case that he loves them. He

moves down stage left and not up stage right. Whatever he doesn't do must be contained and conserved in what he does. In this way every sentence and every gesture signifies a decision; the character remains under observation and is tested.

(*BT* 137)

The 'not-but' strategy embodies Brecht's interest in contradictions as a source of change and revolution, something that we will look at in more detail presently. In order to help actors maintain the type of questioning attitude (towards the actions and remarks of characters) that brings about a 'not-but' moment, Brecht suggests the following aids for defamiliarizing:

- using the third person (not 'I did ... ' but 'He did ... ');
- putting the character's text into the past tense (not 'I'm coming' but 'I came');
- speaking relevant stage directions out loud ('He stood up and exclaimed angrily, not having eaten: ... ' (*BT* 138);
- translating verse into prose;
- translating prose into the actor's native dialect.

Then Brecht asserts (somewhat over-confidently?): 'This composite process leads to [a defamiliarization] of the text in the rehearsals which generally persists in the performance too' (*BT* 138).

But how do these techniques actually relate to the actor's work on the text and final performance? When Brecht's suggestions are taken into a rehearsal space where most of the participants live and breathe capitalist **ideology** and few are familiar with Marxist thought, this question becomes all the more pressing. For instance, there are all manner of things an actor or director can find astounding about a character. But what selection criteria should practitioners use if they are to create, or single out, those responses that will lead to a socially useful 'not-but' – especially if the artist's astonishment is likely to echo rather than illuminate bourgeois attitudes towards a character or situation? And while using the third person and past tense may help the actor to see the character as a construct separate from herself, does it help her to identify the character's socially significant aspects according to an interventionist point of view? What Brecht's essay lacks is a set of guidelines about how to animate these methods through a particular way of looking at play texts and the social world.

A key source of information about modes of viewing is Brecht's model books. Designed as teaching tools, each of these offers invaluable material about the way a particular play was interpreted and staged at the Ensemble. It is here, for example, that Brecht explains that a performance of *Mother Courage* should demonstrate that war is the continuation of business by other means, of no benefit for the 'little people' and positively deadly for the virtuous. As the owner of a canteen wagon during the Thirty Years' War (1618–48), Mother Courage is a *petite bourgeoise*, one of the small fry. She leaves Bamberg in southern Germany in order to follow what Brecht regarded as one of the first large-scale wars brought upon Europe by capitalism. Courage is motivated by the desire to look after herself and her children – Eilif, Swiss Cheese and Kattrin – and her love of making profitable deals. However, the play shows that her support for the war is counterproductive. Not only does she contribute to the slaughter of many young soldiers, but the war claims all three of her children. Brecht presents Courage critically, as someone energetic and intelligent, capable of insight into the reality of war, but who repeatedly chooses to turn a blind eye out of a misguided sense of what best serves her own interests.

In Philip Prowse's 1990 production at The Citizens' Theatre, Glasgow, Courage was played by Glenda Jackson, the famous British actress who went on to become a Labour parliamentarian. Jackson openly remarked that she had avoided reading Brecht's dramatic theories as she considered them 'an excessive kind of baggage' that risked turning the production into 'a museum piece' (Eddershaw 1991: 309). Her Courage was a flawed heroine whose greatest strength and weakness was a lack of imagination. Jackson believed her job was to play the world as Courage sees it (Fogg 1991: 85), rather than to take a sustained questioning attitude towards the character. It is perhaps for this reason that, when asked if there were surprising features in the characterization of Courage, she paused, then, curiously, replied:

> Hm! One line that caused me, the first time I read it, to say 'Oh!' was when she says that her son Eilif was her pet. That surprised me. Yes! I wouldn't have thought she would have voiced it even if she'd felt it.

> (Fogg 1991: 79)

This reply suggests she was unaware that Courage's remark about Eilif should work as a V-effect. That is, the line will shock those spectators under the spell of idealist bourgeois ideology who assume that, regardless of her material circumstances, Courage will be led first and foremost by her role as an egalitarian nurturer of each of her children's psyches.

When Therese Giehse played the role in Brecht's Munich production in 1950, she emphasized Courage's favouritism: she chose to look beyond the character's point of view (as the actress imagined it) and, instead of presenting a comforting vision of motherhood, saw the role of the mother–son relationship in terms of the play's thematic that war and capitalism go hand in hand. Giehse attributed Courage's favouring of Eilif to her belief that initially he looks the most likely to survive and be a good businessman. Not only does he have warrior abilities, but Courage says he 'inherited his father's intelligence: that man could strip the pants off a peasant's ass without his knowing it' (Brecht 1972: 138). Swiss Cheese, on the other hand, is dangerously honest and lacks craftiness, and Kattrin is suicidally compassionate. Her favouritism exposes Courage's belief in the 'survival of the fittest' principle that Brecht held to be part and parcel of the ideology underpinning war and capitalism. It also reveals egalitarian parenting as an ideological veneer that barely conceals a system of hierarchical competition. Guided by her understanding of the play's social/ist meanings, Giehse knew what surprises would be socially significant. Moreover, exaggerating Courage's favouritism is also an example of putting the 'not-but' into operation. One 'not-but' Giehse introduced is the unexpected suggestion that the mother is not egalitarian, but hierarchical, intended to jolt the audience into reflecting on both why it should be unexpected and what its causes are.

Playing contradictions and 'fixing the not-but' are interpretive strategies rather than simply formal devices. While the comparatively mechanical exercise of defamiliarizing a character's lines by employing the third person and past tense is a more immediately accessible technique, and hence a popular one in acting classes, it has a more limited application. In the *Mother Courage* model book, Brecht's description of how he used the technique in rehearsal clarifies how it could stop actors from becoming so emotionally involved in a scene that they could no longer foreground what was significant. For example, he used the method in the emotive episode where Kattrin is shot dead while banging a drum on top of a barn in a desperate bid to alert the Protestant city of Halle to an imminent attack by Catholic troops. In this scene Kattrin's decision is juxtaposed with that of a peasant and his wife who decide that there is nothing they can do except pray (Figure 2.3). Brecht instructed the actors playing the peasants to 'quote' their lines ('said the man/woman') to impress upon them a questioning attitude towards the characters at the very moment when they seek to justify a failure to do as Kattrin does, and act subversively.

Brecht's instructions to the young Carola Braunbock, as the middle-aged peasant woman in this scene, make clear not only how the *Gestus* of showing was implemented but also how it involved a balance between empathizing and critically demonstrating. Braunbock was to take into consideration that her character's toadyism towards the invading soldiers was the result of a life of deprivation and sub-ordination. In the model book Brecht fleshes out features of her background – her miscarriages, the fact that she has walked many times behind the coffins of children who died young, the hard labour of her youth, her beatings at the hands of her parents and husband, her intellectual beatings from clerics – in a manner that recalls the way Stanislavsky encouraged his actors to research and 'get into' their

Figure 2.3 Kattrin runs to alert the citizens of Halle while the peasants pray. Image courtesy of BBA

characters. In the drumming scene, she must witness the physical abuse of her son by soldiers of the army who are preparing to attack the very city where her brother-in-law and his family live. While the play text simply has her beg for mercy and pray for the city, Brecht wanted to show that these were ritualized gestures of defence, acquired through years of practice, against events perpetrated by and against humans, not brought about by chance. Braunbock gave the prayer a hackneyed quality by showing how the woman knelt carefully, one knee at time, made herself comfortable with hands folded over her stomach, and then began to chant in an empty, liturgical manner. The comic edge this gave to her action highlighted Brecht and Braunbock's critical attitude to the efficacy of prayer and counter-balanced any empathetic response to her suffering: her praying was a self-destructive, albeit understandable, response that only aggravated her and her fellow subordinates' condition of alienation. Brecht rein-forced the *Gestus* of showing that the defamiliarizing effect of this comic ritual created by casting a twenty-two-year-old actress as a prematurely aged peasant-woman.

As Brecht discovered, one pitfall of the defamiliarizing gestic approach to character is that it may not be forceful enough to disrupt old viewing habits. He was confronted with the tenacity of these habits when, for example, a significant proportion of even the East German audiences for the *Mother Courage* performances insisted on characterizing the protagonist as a plucky survivor who had been placed in a bleak, chaotic world beyond her control. No doubt the experience of the Nazi regime and of the Second World War con-tributed to the tendency for many to read Courage along these lines. Indeed, a problem with V-effects generally is that, as playful or visually striking devices, they can be all too easily appropriated for commercial purposes. Take, for example, a whisky advertisement featuring a female figure and the word 'HERSTORY' emblazoned across the bottle. In the context of feminist thought, the defamiliarizing use of 'herstory' – a play on 'history' informed by the feminist contention that history (his story) is written by, for and about men – is usually charged by a transformative agenda that, like Marxism, urges readers to change an inequitable economy. However, in the whisky advertise-ment the V-effect hardly fulfils the political function Brecht intended, but simply serves the capitalist purpose of opening up a new market for whisky sales.

HISTORICIZATION: QUESTIONING THE PRESENT THROUGH THE PAST

'Herstory', or feminist retellings of history, also constitutes a more recent application of what Brecht referred to as historicization. In 'Short Description' Brecht presents historicization as a 'crucial technical device' (*BT* 140) and component of *Verfremdung*. Brecht applied the term to a variety of defamiliarizing processes – I shall call them H-effects for short – which aim to both provoke an inquiring attitude towards the present through the past, and challenge dominant versions of history. Here are his key H-effects:

- distancing (contemporary) phenomena by placing them in the past;
- presenting events as the product of historically specific conditions and choices;
- showing differences between the past and present and evidencing change;
- showing similarities between the past and present and urging change;
- revealing received versions of history as the views of the ruling class;
- giving air to suppressed and interventionist histories;
- presenting all versions of history as serving vested interests.

The first of these H-effects is addressed in 'Short Description'. To act with quotation marks is to show that you are *re-presenting* what your character has done some time ago, rather than trying to create a sustained impression of spontaneously living the character's life in the now. 'Short Description' provides instances of quotational acting, drawn from the everyday world and the stage:

- witnesses of an accident demonstrating to newcomers how the victim behaved;
- a facetious person imitating a friend's walk;
- a director or co-actor showing an actor how to play a particular scene.

Brecht always enjoyed what he called the 'marking' or 'indicating' rehearsal (Weber 1967: 103), which produced a similar quotational quality. In these roughly sketched, partial imitations of the play's action, where the performer walks quickly through the actions of the *Fabel* while rapidly quoting the text, the actor and his character are both independently present. For similar reasons Brecht was often drawn to sets that conveyed an unfinished, fragmentary quality, like Teo Otto's design – sketch-like outlines of war-torn buildings, military tents and peasant farmhouses for the Zürich *Mother Courage* in 1941. The quoted milieu also gives the impression of something transient and in flux, changeable through the hands and minds of men and women. Brecht the playwright uses prologues, epilogues, narrators and projected captions foretelling the main action of the scene to create similar H-effects. These techniques help frame the events as historical phenomena that are now under quasi-scientific observation. Brecht hoped that combating the audience's tendency to become absorbed in the staged action in the present would turn the anticipatory 'What's going to happen next?' into the problem-solving 'Why did they do that?'.

Historicization can also involve presenting an event as the product of material conditions and human choices that are specific to a particular historical epoch. As Brecht writes in 'Short Description':

> Historical incidents are unique, transitory incidents associated with particular periods. The conduct of the persons involved in them is not fixed and 'universally human'; it includes elements that have been or may be overtaken by the course of history, and is subject to criticism from the immediately following period's point of view.
>
> (*BT* 140)

Brecht and Carola Braunbock's work on the peasant woman's prayer is an example of quotational acting that presents behaviour as shaped by transitory historical forces. The actress and director clearly signalled that, in their opinion, such routinized behaviour was the product of peasant experience in seventeenth-century Germany – a life of poverty, subordination and indoctrination in a crumbling feudal society – rather than a universally human response. Critical of the tendency of theatre practitioners, particularly when staging plays of other periods, 'to annihilate distance' (*BT* 276), Brecht often paired the demonstration of historical specificity with the foregrounding of differences between the past and the present:

> [W]e must drop our habit of taking the different social structures of past periods, then stripping them of everything that makes them different; so that they all look more or less like our own, which then acquires from this process a certain air of having been there all along, in other words of permanence pure and simple. Instead we must leave them their distinguishing marks and keep their impermanence always before our eyes, so that our own period can be seen to be impermanent too.
>
> (*BT* 190)

By suggesting that the prayer was a problematic response to brutality, the actress-commentator emphasized the *differences* between the outlook of a pious person in a feudal agrarian context and that of a mid-twentieth-century performer in a secular communist context. Her criticism encouraged the audience to consider the pros and cons of the peasant's response to her material conditions. More importantly, it provocatively warned an audience that had participated in Nazism and world war that fatalist abnegation of control should no longer be tolerated. In characteristic Brechtian fashion, the H-effect showing the difference between past and present attitudes came into conflict with the H-effect showing insidious continuities.

Here Brecht's interpretative work is clearly guided by **historical materialism**, the conception of history at the core of Marxist theory. The starting point for that conception is the idea that people are not born with a consciousness that determines their existence, i.e. born with thoughts and feelings, which determine who they will become. Rather, in the first instance their social existence and material life determine their consciousness. In order to meet their material needs for food, shelter, commodities and so on, people must collaborate and this collaboration leads to a mode of production. This mode of production is made up of *forces of production* (e.g. machinery and labour power) and *relations of production* (arrangements regarding who does and who owns what). The owners of the means of production constitute the ruling class. In eighteenth-century Europe the main mode of production was still agriculture and the means of production were owned by the landed aristocracy supported by the crown. Together, the monarchy and nobility controlled the land, agricultural technology, peasant labourers and the legal and political superstructure. Their material position determined their own consciousness, encouraging them to believe they had God-given rights to property and wealth and a paternal duty to provide the less fortunate with the means of survival. Peasants, in an exploited position and obliged to carry out largely manual labour, had a very different idea of who they were. So the causal chain looks something like this: I eat and drink – I work socially – I am of a certain social class – these material and social activities shape my thought, which in turn shapes my activities and my sense of who I am.

According to many of Marx and Engels's pronouncements on historical materialism – and this part of the theory is hotly debated by Marxists and non-Marxists alike – the development of productive forces brings about the birth of a new mode of production and new class relations. For example, the development of industrial machinery in the eighteenth century led to a collision between the landed gentry and the owners of these new productive forces, the **bourgeoisie**. The result was the replacement of agricultural feudalism with capitalism, and the replacement of the old antagonism between the nobility and peasantry with a conflict between the bourgeoisie and **proletariat**. These economic and social changes are progressive in so far as they gradually usher in societies with greater productive capacity, setting the conditions for human liberation from subsistence and class rule. Historical materialism's vision of the relationship between economics and consciousness, and of the emancipatory potential of material change, echoes throughout Brecht's historicist theatre. However, as a cultural activist Brecht was also drawn to the thought of Marxists, such as Karl Korsch, who argued that social transformation requires a synthesis of theoretical critique and intellectual agitation with more direct modes of economic and political action (Giles 1997: 92–3). Brecht's interest in intellectual activism can be found in his attention to the way ideology is one force that shapes the behaviour of his characters and spectators. It also inflects the way he encourages actors and directors to assert the power of human consciousness through 'fixing the not-but' – Läuffer, the maid and the peasant woman do *not* rebel, *but* acquiesce – which highlights moments of choice.

Both the *Mother Courage* play text and the Ensemble productions repeatedly foreground the materialist and utilitarian nature of their take on history. Brecht's interpretation of the Thirty Years' War as motivated by dynastic interests and territorial greed rather than religious beliefs is overtly Marxist. This partisan treatment, for Keith Dickson 'an exaggeration rather than a falsification' (Dickson 1978:

97), is clearly designed to serve Brecht's political intervention in his contemporary world. Brecht initially intended the play, written in exile immediately after Germany's invasion of Poland in September 1939, as a way of alerting his Scandinavian hosts, Denmark and Sweden, to Hitler's imperial ambitions and the folly of thinking they could make a profit from war without getting burnt. When he staged the play a decade later in war-torn East Berlin, the pressing concern was to lay before an audience who had lived through Nazi Germany the possibility of choice – to serve a genuine (communist) collective, or to pursue a misguided sense of self-interest or national glory. Brecht's theatre not only wears its partisan approach to history on its sleeve, it exposes supposedly neutral versions of history as serving ruling-class interests. For example, in *Mother Courage*, contrary to the tendency of historians to focus on the political, religious and military 'heroes' and their manoeuvres, he foregrounds plebeian perspectives. One of the play's most memorable inversions of received history is the setting upstage of the funeral march for General Tilly, the Bavarian commander of the Catholic league, while Courage and her daughter do a canteen inventory downstage: 'It's a shame about the general – socks: twenty-two pairs – I hear he was killed by accident' (Brecht 1972: 177). Today, in a context where communism rather than the (capitalist) state has withered away and narratives of progress and liberation are regarded with increased scepticism, aspects of Brecht's partisan approach to history are in need of revision. Nevertheless, his entertaining and provocative H-effects continue to provide interventionist theatre with useful tools for questioning tradition and celebrating change.

THE MODERN THEATRE IS THE EPIC THEATRE

Brecht's interest in the intersection of art and history resonates in the very phrase most commonly applied to his entire body of theory and practice: 'epic theatre'. The term 'epic' stands for a mode of literature and performance that is distinguished by an emphasis on *telling* something about the past, as opposed to drama with its present-tense, dialogue-based *showing*, and the lyric genre that emphasizes its author's subjective thoughts and feelings. Of course, literary art – and Brecht's work is a case in point – has often combined aspects of two or all of these modes. For example, the chorus in ancient Greek drama is an epic element, something Brecht adapted in his **Lehrstücke** ('learning-plays'). At the time of Aristotle's *Poetics*, the epic was also a distinct genre – a long, narrative poem recited by a solo performer, retelling heroic tales of national history or legend. Although Brecht does not discuss the ancient epic in any detail, his modern epic theatre certainly echoes and inverts aspects of its form and function. For example, both types of epic use episodic narrations of the past to educate and stir to action in the present. But whereas the ancient form often promoted aristocratic values, Brecht's theatre tended to reveal the way oppressive traditions served vested interests.

Brecht began regularly applying the phrase 'epic theatre' to his experiments in 1926, and there are a number of reasons why the term 'epic' emerged as an apt way of describing his new playwriting and staging. Towards the end of the war and during the early upheavals surrounding the foundation of the Weimar Republic in 1918, the hyperbolic lyricism of expressionism was a dominant force in avantgarde performance. However, due to factors including the need to build a new society, the stabilization of the economy, rationalizing tendencies brought about by the intensification of mass production techniques during the war, and the pedagogical strategies of Germany's Communist Party, a more matter-of-fact and utilitarian approach took hold in the arts. The emergent style and structure of feeling was referred to as *Neue Sachlichkeit*, ('New Sobriety'or 'New Objectivity'). Many of the art forms of New Sobriety, as well as the **agitprop** companies of the Communist Party, attempted to give a critical appraisal of social processes, often adapting journalistic approaches and new mass media technology. In a context where the behaviour and attitude of a reporter was upheld as exemplary, it is hardly surprising that Brecht and his famous colleague, Erwin Piscator, founder of a revolutionary documentary theatre, began to reanimate the term 'epic' and inflect it with new meanings.

If the term remained important to Brecht during the rest of his career it was principally because it connoted a type of art that contains reportage as well as giving prominence to narration and an observing narrator figure who draws attention to the causes of events. These features, Brecht argued, would lend themselves to a theatre of the modern age that wished to present the complexities of class war with the help of the new sciences, and in 1935 he wrote:

The stage began to be instructive.

> Oil, inflation, war, social struggles, the family, religion, wheat, the meat market, all became subjects for theatrical representation. Choruses enlightened the spectator about facts unknown to him. Films showed a montage of events from all over the world. Projections added statistical material. And as the 'background' came to the front of the stage so people's activity was subjected to criticism.

> *(BT* 71–2)

Secondly, he found the episodic structure of the ancient epic, and related forms like Shakespeare's chronicle plays, ideal for presenting an interrupted, not necessarily linear action-flow, and similarly, therefore, the individual's alterability. Thirdly, many of Brecht's plays, especially *Mother Courage* and *Life of Galileo*, also contain echoes of the epic tendency towards flux and breadth rather than unity, in so far as they shun the unities of time, place and action to explore the diverse exploits of multiple characters over a great sweep of time and place. Finally, terms such as 'epic' and 'non-Aristotelian' helped Brecht to clarify his contestation of the way the major theatre of his day lacked epic qualities and, after Aristotle, prioritized empathetic present-tense or 'dramatic' theatre.

'Epic theatre' is thus an umbrella term for all those technical devices and methods of interpretation – from showing the *Gestus* to V- and H-effects – that contribute to an analytic narrative perspective. But it also embraces structural issues such as the organization of space and time so that a particular view of the individual and society is communicated. These structural issues are memorably raised in Brecht's 'Notes to the Opera *The Rise and Fall of the City of Mahagonny*', especially its (in)famous opposition of the dramatic and epic forms of theatre. It is to this that we now turn.

'NOTES TO THE OPERA *THE RISE AND FALL OF THE CITY OF MAHAGONNY*' (1930)

In the 'Notes to the Opera', first published in the autumn of 1930, Brecht introduced what he called 'culinary' art – selected and shaped by capitalist apparatuses such as the opera, theatre and press to provide easily consumable fodder for the entertainment machine. The notes suggest that, in a society where artists do not own their means of production (the apparatuses), they will be alienated from their art and it in turn will remain merchandise. According to the logic of Brecht's argument, even his own avant-garde experiments with form, content and audience reception risked falling prey to the commodification process if the controlling apparatuses remain untouched. At about this time Brecht was testing another apparatus through his *Lehrstücke*. While many of these were performed in mainstream theatres, they were primarily intended to be workshopped without a public performance and in non-theatrical spaces such as schools. That is, they were conceived as educational tools for the direct benefit of their professional and amateur participants. As is often the case in a workshop or rehearsal, the participants were both performers and observer-critics, now playing a character, now reflecting on that character and modifying it through a replaying, now sitting on the sidelines observing other characters and relationships. Brecht's interest in developing a new art of '**spectActing**' achieves one of its fullest expressions in the *Lehrstück* workshop – not the passive consumerism of culinary art, but an active role on the part of both actors and audience.

In the 'Notes to the Opera', rather than discussing an alternative apparatus, he looks to revolutionize the old one from within by shifting from the tendencies of dramatic theatre to those of epic theatre. He provides a table that contrasts the two forms, adding this cautionary note to users:

> This table does not show absolute antitheses but mere shifts of accent. In a communication of fact, for instance, we may choose whether to stress the element of emotional suggestion or that of plain rational argument.
>
> (*BT* 37)

Despite this warning, the table is repeatedly misinterpreted as a set of rigid oppositions. Prior to publishing the essay in the 1938 edition of his collected works, Brecht made some significant alterations to the table and it is the modified version that is given on page 80. It is worth comparing this 1938 table (which appears in German in *Werke* 1991: 85) with the one appearing in John Willett's translation of the 1935 essay (*BT* 37). While the logic of Brecht's list is not immediately apparent, the oppositions relate to crucial aspects of his theatre. I have added a third column, a code to help readers see which items relate to Brecht's general world view (W), to his views of dramatic structure and presentation (S) and to ways he wants the spectator to receive and engage with his work/message (R). Often these items overlap, hence for example S/R.

Dramatic form of theatre	Epic form of theatre	Code
The stage 'embodies' an event	The stage narrates an event	S/R
implicates the spectator in an action and wears down his capacity for action	turns the spectator into an observer, but arouses his capacity for action	R
provides him with feelings	forces him to take decisions	R
gives him experiences	gives him knowledge	R
the spectator is involved in an action	he is made to face the action	R
suggestion is used	arguments are used	S/R
the instinctive feelings are preserved	brought to the point of recognition	R
the human being is taken for granted	the human being is the object of the inquiry	W
he is unalterable	he is alterable and able to alter	W
eyes on the finish	eyes on the course	S/R
one scene makes another	each scene for itself	S/W
the course of the events is linear	in curves	S/W
natura non facit saltus (nature does not leap)	facit saltus (nature leaps)	S/W
the world as it is	the world as it becomes	W
what the human being should do	what the human being must do	W
his drives and desires	his motives	W
thought determines being	social being determines thought	W

A noticeable difference in the 1938 table (my own translation) is the absence of the opposition 'feeling/reason', which suggests that Brecht had grown weary of the mistaken suggestion that his theatre banished emotion and empathy.

In what follows I will be dealing mainly with structural issues raised by the table, bearing in mind that they cannot be isolated from the other aspects. For example, Brecht argued that dramatic theatre's approach to structure ('one scene makes another', 'linear development', 'eyes on the finish') embodied the philosophy that 'thought determines being' and the fatalist idea that human nature is unalterable, that the destiny of a character lies within that character's given self and must be only unfolded, that character is not formed through social interaction so much as by its given mind and psyche. In dramatic theatre, the events of the plot are dovetailed in such a way that they create a plummeting, arrow-like motion towards moments of emotional interest wherein something about the psyche of the character is revealed. It is a structure with implications for reception, as it encourages the spectator to concentrate on where a character is heading and to get caught up in the protagonists' suspense-laden passage towards their pre-given end.

By contrast, Brecht's use of episodic structure ('each scene for itself') is an artistic response to the philosophical view that 'social being determines thought' and 'man is alterable and able to alter'. In order to illustrate his view that the individual operates in a world of shifting forces – she is changed by those forces and can, in her turn, respond and change them too – Brecht used a type of montage approach, juxtaposing relatively autonomous scenes, each analogous to a force field and containing its own mini-episodes. Rather than dovetailing the scenes, and episodes within them, he places them in opposition and inserts interruptive devices – a reflective song or direct address – that encourage the audience to have their 'eyes on the course', on means rather than simply ends.

Brecht's sparse comments on structure in the 'Notes to the Opera' can leave the reader wondering how all this theory relates to performance practice. Again, the work of the Berliner Ensemble provides some clues. Weigel's Mother Courage plotted leaps from one comportment to its polar opposite. For instance, her 'leap' from scene 6 to 7 highlighted Courage's contradictory attitude toward war. At the conclusion of scene 6, the character damns the war: the actress showed the enraged attitude of a mother who has just bandaged her daughter's bleeding forehead, a wound that Kattrin received while gathering supplies for the canteen (Figure 2.4). A few seconds later Weigel re-entered for scene 7, singing her praise of the war. The

Figure 2.4 Mother Courage damns the war. Image courtesy of BBA

actress looked markedly different, too: striding exuberantly alongside a well-stocked wagon, she was wearing rings on her fingers and a chain of silver coins round her neck (Figure 2.5). In the 1960 film version of this production, Weigel marched as she sang and, at a reference in her song to war victory, made a gesture that recalled the Nazi *Sieg Heil* ('Hail victory!') salute. The impact of her economic prosperity was plain to see. Weigel highlighted contradictions not only between scenes but also within single episodes. For example, as she played Courage cursing war Weigel gathered together the very supplies that had cost her daughter so dearly. Mechanically, she ran flour through her hands to test its grade. This complex of gestures foregrounded the 'caring mother – calculating merchant' contradiction and helped present Courage as a dynamic unity of unstable opposites.

The Ensemble company further scored this episodic structure with isolated, interruptive gestures and tableaux. Weigel devised several memorable 'freeze-framing' gestures. One was the snapping shut of her leather purse as she sealed every business deal. The finality of the sharp, audible click and the repetition of the hand movement – marking at once her joy at making the deal and her constant need to ensure the means of economic subsistence – isolated and defamiliarized an ordinary, mundane gesture. It emphasized her enjoyment at the conclusion of a deal and her need continually to ensure and

Figure 2.5 Mother Courage sings the war's praises. Photo by Ruth Berlau,
© Ruth Berlau/Hilda Hoffmann, image courtesy of BBA

safeguard the means of economic subsistence. Brecht extended this focus on the pictorial quality of gesture to the movements of an entire group through his approach to the sculptural organization of individuals and groups in relation to others. One of the first steps he took when organizing a production was to commission his designer to provide sketches of possible *Arrangements*, or groupings and movements of characters in accordance with the *Fabel*. The Ensemble scenographer, Karl von Appen, began his work 'by trying to narrate a play optically' (Baugh, in Thomson and Sacks 1994: 247). When it came to working with the actors, the early stages were dominated by *Stellproben*, literally 'position' rehearsals. In his study of twentieth-century directorial methods, David Richard Jones contrasts Brecht's question in rehearsal, 'What's the position?', with Stanislavsky's catch-cry, 'I don't believe it!' (Jones 1986: 87). During rehearsals and often prior to performance at the Berliner Ensemble, the crucial positionings were scrutinized with the aid of photos taken at rehearsals. Brecht sought to enhance the separateness, and hence clarity, of each picture by encouraging actors to retain their significant groupings, rather than move about in order to attract audience attention, and not to speak while moving from one position or space to another. Brecht's tableaux aesthetic – an insistence on disciplined ensemble work and the separation of parts – owes something to the film-maker's freeze-framing technique, and gave the Ensemble's productions the quality of a film strip, each picture relatively autonomous while at the same time embedded within the course of events.

It is through a separation and conflict of parts that Brecht sought to create a theatre of flux as distinct from a dramatic theatre of fusion. In 'Notes to the Opera' he makes clear that his call for 'a radical separation of the elements' stems from his antipathy towards a certain approach to unity:

> So long as the expression 'Gesamtkunstwerk' (or 'integrated work of art') means that the integration is a muddle, so long as the arts are supposed to be 'fused' together, the various elements will all be equally degraded, and each will act as a mere 'feed' to the rest. The process of fusion extends to the spectator, who gets thrown into the melting pot too and becomes a passive (suffering) part of the total work of art.
>
> (*BT* 37–8)

In dramatic theatre, parts are brought into a synthesis that leaves no room for analysis. By contrast, Brecht tried to keep elements such as music, text and scenography relatively independent of one another. In *The Threepenny Opera*, first performed in 1928, the songs were isolated from the action both in terms of content and by formal means such as darkening the stage so that only the singers and upstage orchestra and barrel-organ were illuminated. The musical setting of the text was also imbued with the principle of separation and contrast. For example, the simple melody of the famous 'Mac the Knife' ballad, based around a C major triad, is set against the ballad's lyrics about the exploits of a Jack-the-Ripper style killer. While the melody helps create the charm and reassuring solidity of Macheath's comportment as a gentleman businessman, the other elements point to the criminal nature of his activities as a pimp and thief. Echoes of the separation principle are to be found whenever Brecht insists on difference and division: between actor and character, character and spectator, telling and showing, doing and observing. The separations do not banish unity per se, but replace a static synthetic model with a more unstable or dialectical unity of contradictions.

DIALECTICS IN THE THEATRE

Contradiction was always a vital feature of Brecht's theatre. However, as he became increasingly familiar with Marxism he came to view the idea of contradiction in accordance with the philosophy of **dialectical materialism**. The concept of dialectics features in many of Brecht's writings, particularly on politics and philosophy, but towards the end of his life he began to prioritize it by replacing the phrase 'epic theatre' with the phrase 'dialectical theatre'. In the early 1950s Brecht argued that it was time to discard the concept of the 'epic'. While it had strengthened 'the narrative element that is part of the theatre in general', it had been 'too inflexibly opposed to the concept of the dramatic' and had become a formal concept that could just as well be applied to non-Marxist authors (*BT* 276, 281). By contrast, 'dialectics' better conveyed the political significance of contradictions with regard to the content, form and reception of his work.

At the heart of dialectical thinking is the belief that contradictions are the source of change and progressive development. Brecht's fascination with the dynamics of dialogue and debate, of moving towards more truthful or useful ideas by pitting conflicting arguments against one another, is an example of his interest in dialectical logic. His presentation of the class tensions between Läuffer, the tutor, and his aristocratic patrons is an example of his interest in dialectical materialism. According to this philosophy, the driving force behind the progressive history of society – its rise from primitive communism, via the slave system, then feudalism and capitalism, to socialism and advanced communism – is the basic contradiction between forces and relations of production. Under the capitalist system this contradiction consists in a tension between the social means of production (large workshops and factories) and private ownership of these means. According to Marxist dialectics, the basic contradiction in turn generates the conflict between the working and the capitalist classes, an antagonistic opposition involving economic inequities. This class conflict is resolved through the revolt of the workers and their instigation of a classless society. The workers' negation of capitalism does not involve a total rejection of the past, but a synthesis of what was best about the old system – the advanced forces of production that can ensure material well-being for everyone – with a new system of public ownership. Contradictions will continue to emerge under communism but, being free from antagonism, they can be resolved through critical discussion.

Some of Brecht's procedures for showing the necessity and possibility of change have a remarkable resemblance to the dialectical laws of motion and development drawn up by Engels. His presentation of characters and relationships as constituting an unstable unity of contradictions is one example. This is related to the law of the interpenetration of opposites according to which the opposite sides of a contradiction – say, master and slave – cannot exist independently. Writing about the role of dialectics in Brecht's theatre, Peter Brooker describes the V-effect as involving a process that mirrors Engels's negation law (Brooker 1988: 83–4). According to this law, any negative force is negated in a process of historical development that conserves something of the negated elements. In the case of the V-effect, whatever is 'natural' and familiar (a peasant woman praying for the safety of relatives during war) is 'negated', made to appear strange (through a comic ritualization of the prayer). But then, in the negation of the negation, the phenomenon is returned in a transformed state, with new meaning, a contradictory entity (victim and victimizer) capable of different behaviour under changed economic circumstances.

BRECHT'S SOCIALIST REALISM: IMITATION MEETS EXPERIMENTATION

Dialectical thinking also informed Brecht's preference for his own form of 'socialist realism' as opposed to 'naturalism'. While his theatre is often presented as the antithesis of late nineteenth-century naturalism and Stanislavsky's psychological realism, it actually preserves what he regarded as its progressive features. These include its careful observation of the material world and its concern with the relation between character and social environment. In the 1940s Brecht included observation and imitation games in his exercises for actors, and in the 1950s he increasingly used Stanislavsky's method of fleshing out a character's given circumstances – taking care, of course, to distinguish the socially significant. For, as he makes clear in 'Short Description', the quoting actor should always preserve the 'full human and concrete shape' of a remark and the 'full substance of a human gesture even though it now represents a copy' (*BT* 138). However, Brecht thought Stanislavsky's approach to imitation was limited:

> His naturalistic works, then, consist of elaborately detailed pictures of society. They're like those deep-dug soil samples which botanists put on the laboratory bench and examine …. What he cared about was *naturalness*, and as a result everything in his theatre seemed far too natural for anyone to pause and go into it thoroughly. You don't normally examine your own home or your own eating habits, do you? … The man who drops a pebble hasn't begun representing the law of gravity, you know; nor has the man who merely gives an exact description of its fall.
>
> (Brecht 1965: 23–4)

What Brecht's *Messingkauf* dramaturg is getting at here is that, while Stanislavsky reproduces concrete details from different societies, he provides neither any analysis of, nor opinion about, the structures and relations that lie beyond direct, immediate experience.

In his essay 'The Popular and the Realistic' (1938) Brecht defined a realist as a revolutionary who exposes false pictures of reality for the benefit of the proletarian cause:

Realistic means:

> revealing the causal complex of society/unmasking the ruling viewpoints as the viewpoints of the rulers/ writing from the standpoint of the class that has in readiness the broadest solutions for the most urgent difficulties besetting human society/ emphasizing the factor of development/concretely and making it possible to abstract.
>
> (Brecht 2003: 205–6)

Brecht used the term 'concrete' when speaking of realism to mean, first, that art should refer to material actuality and be concerned with socio-historically specific and particular instances. Second, it must capture the lively variety of these instances, the restless movement of contradictions and disharmonies. The realist makes it possible to abstract what is significant from the concrete through artistic methods such as selection, isolation and magnification. In his essay 'The Street Scene' (also 1938), Brecht clarifies how the realist performer can combine working concretely while enabling abstraction in the related pairing of 'naturalness' and 'stylization'. His street scene – a basic model of epic theatre – consists of a bystander talking to a crowd that has gathered about an accident he has just witnessed and helping them to assess causal factors and outcomes. His 'performance' provides a primitive example of how to combine naturalness and stylization. For example, when he responds to a crowd member's comment by replaying how the accident victim stepped off the kerb with his right rather than his left foot, he achieves stylization 'by paying exact attention this time to his movements, executing them carefully, probably in slow motion' (*BT* 126). His *Gestus* of showing results in the distortion of time and spatial movement. However, his demonstration retains naturalness and concreteness in a couple of ways. First, it mirrors the contradictory flux of life: demonstrator and subject are not fused into a non-contradictory unity, but sustain a tension. Second, the demonstrator refers to the observed gestures of a historical entity.

The actor takes the bystander's performance one step further by combining imitation with highly entertaining experimentation. Brecht's vigorous defence of artistic experimentation is one of the features that distinguish his realism from the stultifying aspects of Soviet Socialist Realism, the prescribed artistic practice that emerged from the First

Soviet Writer's conference in 1934. Its aim was to make art intelligible to the people, and hence it involved the exclusion of anything abstract or removed from ordinary experience. Brecht's positive attitude towards formal experimentation stemmed from his belief that the political function of art was the revelation of contradictory social reality through the pleasurable manipulation of form. Moreover, by employing new techniques, the realist not only reflected historical change, but also provided a model of revolutionary experimentation by showing how reality could be altered through artistic shaping. The masks in Brecht's production of *The Caucasian Chalk Circle* (1953) exemplify the resulting collision of imitative and defamiliarizing modes of representation. While some of the masks were modelled on the grotesque types from *commedia dell'Arte* and Asian theatre, Brecht tried to ensure that each was individualized and, rather than being fantastically absurd, drew attention to a type of human. What Brecht's dialectical socialist realism gives rise to is a theatre that is unique in its rich unity of mimesis and imagination.

CONCLUSION

Brecht made it clear that his theatre was tailored for a Marxist practitioner when he wrote provocatively that, unless 'the actor is satisfied to be a parrot or a monkey he must master our period's knowledge of human social life by himself joining in the war of the classes' (*BT* 196). As this chapter has demonstrated, after 1926 Brecht's art and socialist politics went hand in hand. So, can his theory and staging *only* have relevance for a Marxist theatre? Is Brecht's theatre meaningless to the non-Marxist? Or the student who despairs of ever coming to grips with his world view? And, frankly, is it worth it when many features of dialectical and historical materialism – the utopian predictions, the tendency to place productive technology as the principal cause of social development, the prioritization of class over other issues such as race and gender – seem flawed and out of touch with the contemporary world? The short answer is, if you are moti-vated by the possibility of changing thought and behaviour, it is definitely worth engaging with Brecht. And the first thing he would insist you change, of course, would be the shortcomings of his own worldview.

It has been the aim of this chapter to open up Brecht's strategies in such a way that they can be grasped and modified by a broad range of practitioners. For Brecht has a lot to offer any artist, teacher and/or learner interested in questioning seemingly fixed ways of organizing, viewing and representing the world. By 'fixed', I mean treated as 'given', 'natural', 'normal', 'familiar', 'assumed to be true' and thus 'unquestioningly perpetuated'. The desire to 'unfix' permeates Brecht's attempt to demonstrate *how*, *why* and *for whom* certain behaviours, relations and representations are constructed. Moreover, he seeks to show the mutability of such constructs. In a globalized context characterized by an expanding welter of images and power networks, Brecht's endeavours remain a springboard for all those game enough to question the way things seem to be. I leave the last words to Brecht, who had a talent for putting his own case:

> [I] cannot say that the dramatic writing which I call 'non-aristotelian', and the epic style of acting that goes with it, represent the only solution. However, one thing has become quite plain: the present-day world can only be described to present-day people if it is described as capable of transformation.
>
> (*BT* 274)

3

THE CAUCASIAN CHALK CIRCLE: A MODEL PRODUCTION

PROLOGUE: A MODEL

The Berliner Ensemble's 1954 staging of *The Caucasian Chalk Circle* in East Berlin was a spectacular embodiment of Brecht's passion for collective creativity. One of the last productions of his own work that Brecht undertook, it vividly demonstrated what had become his trademarks, especially his Marxist approach to text and *mise-en-scène*. Like all his stagings it was characterized both by the consolidation of earlier innovations and by new departures that marked his receptiveness to the immediate political context and love of artistic experimentation. Not only did the production continue his technique of expressing contradictory reality by combining divergent modes of performance, but it also ushered in a new experiment with mixed genre. The *Chalk Circle* is an intriguingly hybrid form, bringing together Brecht's established practice of satirizing class-based society with what for him was the relatively unfamiliar strategy of modifying 'happy ending' traditions in order to celebrate the pathway to a just and communitarian society.

Like none other of his productions, this one showcased Brecht's delight in mixing old and new artistry in order to make a social point. Here Brechtian **epic theatre** collided with **Aristotelian** dramatic techniques, and ancient Greek and Asian, medieval and folk art were brought into dialogue with various forms of contemporary realist performance. While the play contains numerous clues about the type of dialectical staging Brecht envisaged, many interpreters emphasize its **dramatic theatre** features without considering their relation to antithetical elements or to Brecht's transformative politics. As a result, this much-performed text is often read and staged as a melodrama in which justice and love appear 'dependent on the quirks of fortune' rather than on social change brought about by human agency (White 1978: 158). In this chapter I offer an alternative interpretation that demonstrates why Brecht regarded his political performance strategies as embedded in the text – an opinion he expressed early in rehearsals when everything seemed to be running of its own accord, leading him to exclaim that the only possible way of staging it was implicit in the play (BBA 944/17). Of course Brecht was aware that his work could and would be interpreted in diverse ways, but he was clearly surprised at how readily it lent itself to the ethos and methods of the Ensemble. As this company's practice is still not widely understood, I shall try to show how the Brecht collective carefully and playfully animated the text in accordance with their politics.

That Brecht regarded the production as an exemplary experiment is evident from the fact that he commissioned Hans Bunge, and many other directorial assistants, to create a *Modellbuch* ('model book'). When reading this chapter it is important to keep in mind that for Brecht a model was not a definitive 'classic' to be slavishly and eternally imitated. Rather, it was a clarifying example of his company's experimental methods and their relation to a particular historical moment, a guide whose wisdom should be tested afresh in each new circumstance. While the model book was never finalized, the extensive documentation of the staging through rehearsal notes, recordings and photographs offers us an invaluable insight into why and how Brecht and his numerous collaborators – assistant director Manfred Wekwerth, scenographer Karl von Appen, costume and mask designer Kurt Palm, composer Paul Dessau, actors, dramaturges and other **spectActors** on and off stage – created a production rich with socially significant gestures and groupings. In our own political environments it is likely that some of the Ensemble's strategies will no longer be appropriate tools for resisting oppression and forging new types of community. But in order to make that judgement we first have to understand the old wisdom.

SOURCE MATERIALS

There are a number of ways of getting to know the *Chalk Circle* model. Given that Brecht was a playwright-director, versions of the play text are an important source. The first drafts, which he wrote in collaboration primarily with Ruth Berlau, were completed during his American exile in 1944. He made (mainly stylistic) changes throughout the rest of his life, publishing different editions, including a 1954 text directly influenced by his experiences in directing the play. For English-language readers the best-known and readily accessible translations are:

1 Revised translation by James and Tania Stern with W.H. Auden, with commentary and notes by Hugh Rorrison, London: Methuen, 1984, 2005.
2 Revised English version by Eric Bentley, Minneapolis: University of Minnesota Press, 1999.

In this chapter I will be quoting from the Stern and Auden translation – a reworking of their 1944–6 version – partly because it is clearly informed by Brecht's work on the text in the light of the Ensemble production. Moreover, Brecht was much enamoured of poet W.H. Auden's rendering of the lyrics, which to my mind powerfully convey the artistry of the original's poetry. For better or worse, Brecht also had considerable input into this translation. While he was dissatisfied with the prose sections, later encouraging Eric Bentley and Maya Apelman to attempt a new translation, James Stern did carry out the changes suggested by Brecht before the first Stern and Auden version went to print (Lyon 1980: 128–9).

Whichever copy of the play you are able to locate, it is worth checking the year of the German version it is based on and whether it contains the opening 'Prologue', which Brecht renamed 'The Struggle for the Valley' shortly before his death. By creating a new title, and by numbering it the first of six scenes, Brecht clearly indicated that he wanted this utopian presentation of Georgian agricultural collectives building a socialist future in the wake of the Second World War to be treated as an integral part of the play. For political and historical reasons this frame play has often been omitted, both in print and on stage. On some rare occasions Brecht himself authorized its omission, a judgement made in order to ensure both his own survival and the public dissemination of his work during the Cold War. Yet all his extant comments about the valley scene suggest he regarded it as crucial to the play's vision of social change.

Methuen's 1984 edition of the preferred translation contains both the 'Prologue' and politically astute commentary from Hugh Rorrison, which is clearly informed by a close acquaintance with rehearsal documents, as well as a helpful collection of production photos. Alfred D. White (1978) presents an equally insightful interpretation of German-language materials on the production, while John Fuegi (1987) offers very helpful information and translations from key primary sources. Here, these guides are supplemented with my own research at the Bertolt Brecht Archive (BBA) into the numerous first-hand accounts made by Bunge and his colleagues. I also draw on Brecht's notes about the text, which appear in translation in volume 7 of the *Collected Plays* (Brecht 1976), and on two German volumes about the production edited by Werner Hecht (1966, 1985). The latter includes reviews, as well as commentaries from collaborators such as the actress Angelika Hurwicz, who played Grusha, the play's heroine. Even if you do not read German, Hecht's volumes are valuable for their numerous photographs, sketches and set and costume designs. Further helpful visual material on the production can be found in the book Hurwicz produced together with photographer Gerda Goedhart (1964), the pictorial Brecht biography by Ernst and Renate Schumacher (1981) and Friedrich Dieckmann's richly illustrated volume on Karl von Appen's scenographic work at the Ensemble (1971).

This chapter not only reconstructs the production from archive materials, but it also interprets them very differently from writers such as Fuegi. While Fuegi reminds us that many of the source materials surrounding the production are or could be edited records, tidied up for posterity, his interpretation of these records and the additional information he has discovered is underpinned by assumptions that lead him to dismiss Brecht's politics. Consequently Fuegi sees Brecht as an innate genius as well as a contradictory and cruel psychosexual entity, whose 'essential self', rather than his passion for social change, was the shaping force for his art. This assumption explains why Fuegi treats Brecht's interest in contradiction as primarily the product of an ingrained emotional volatility, evidenced supposedly by Brecht's sudden mood changes during rehearsal, and by a major shift in his sexual affections during the production. A further assumption informing Fuegi's commentary is the belief that dramatic theatre – one that prioritizes action over narration, encouraging identification, **empathy** and emotional stimulation – is mature theatre. For him the presence of dramatic elements in the *Chalk Circle* production makes it 'the lovely butterfly of dramatic art' rather than the plain caterpillar of Brecht's early epic theatre (Fuegi 1987: 149–50; 167). In contrast to Fuegi's emphasis on the *Chalk Circle*'s dramatic elements, this chapter considers their dialogue with epic demonstration and how they served Brecht's social(ist) agenda in a particular historical moment.

PLOTTING NEW MODELS OF PRODUCTIVITY

A model of dialectical art, the 1954 staging also presented Brecht's preferred model of economic production. A brief overview of the play's plot makes apparent that this theatre event addressed the issue of how we can create ways of producing ourselves and our society that are more empowering and just for all. The opening frame play, set in a decimated Caucasian village in the aftermath of the Second World War, depicts a meeting between delegates of the Galinsk goat-breeding kolchos (or collective farm) and delegates from the neighbouring Rosa Luxemburg fruit-growing kolchos. They discuss the settlement and use of a valley previously farmed by the Galinsk members and located in the Caucasus, a range of mountains between the Black Sea and the Caspian Sea. We learn that during Hitler's invasion the goat-herders were forced to move further east and the fruit-growers had to become fighters, moving to the hills to defend the terrain. Now the Galinsk kolchos wish to resettle the beloved homeland where they have lived for centuries. According to the old laws, the land is theirs. However, in a bid to make the defended homeland even more fertile, the Rosa Luxemburg kolchos have devised an irrigation project that will increase 'their' orchards tenfold and even make possible the introduction of vineyards – but only if the disputed valley is included. After a peaceful debate presided over by an Expert from the Reconstruction Commission, including a cheese-tasting moment that confirms the goat-herders are still producing a calibre product even in their new homeland, all delegates agree to the orchard plan.

To celebrate the visit of their former neighbours, in the evening the fruit-growers and the epic singer Arkadi Cheidze stage 'The Chalk Circle', a play directly relevant to their earlier debate about ownership and justice. Despite the many demands of post-war reconstruction, the farmers put aside considerable time and resources for the performance. The state representative is encouraged to pay the same respect to art. When the busy Expert inquires whether the play can be shortened, the Singer answers with a firm 'No'. Ironically, for the Berlin production Brecht did shorten his play, aware that nearly four hours' running time would have made the public transport logistics a nightmare for his audience. Even the edited version demanded a serious commitment of time, from both the live audiences that witnessed it in East Berlin, London and Moscow, and the practitioners whose 125 rehearsals were spread from November 1953 to the premiere on 7 October 1954. In addition, the production demanded a serious financial commitment from the East German government, as it required a cast of about sixty performers to play approximately 150 roles as well as needing musicians and elaborate scenography. The Singer's response to the Expert offers a strategic reminder that theatre itself is an important productive activity that can demonstrate how the collective management of ideas, materials and human relations is able to produce a garden in bloom for all.

Introduced by the Singer as an old legend 'derived from the Chinese' (8), 'The Chalk Circle' is set in Grusinia, medieval Georgia. It has musical accompaniment, contains epic songs and is performed with the help of the old masks supplied by Arkadi Cheidze and his travelling musical troupe. The play comprises two fictional stories that both take place in the wake of a palace uprising, instigated by a group of princes who overthrow the Grand Duke and his Governor. The first story, which starts in scene 2, depicts the downfall and beheading of Governor Georgi Abashvili (Figure 3.1), as well as his wife Natella's hasty departure from the city of Nukha – so hasty she leaves her only child behind. Baby Michael is discovered by Grusha Vachnadze, a palace kitchen-maid, just after her fiancé, soldier Simon Chachawa, has been ordered to accompany Natella on her flight. After much reflection, Grusha decides to rescue the child and flees with it into the country. In scene 3, after an unsuccessful attempt to leave Michael with a peasant couple, and with soldiers in hot pursuit, at considerable risk to herself she decides to become his parent, continuing the

Figure 3.1 Siegfried Kilian as the Governor, Georgi Abashvili, and Helene Weigel as the Governor's wife. Photo by Abraham Pisarek, © Stadtmuseum Berlin

dangerous journey to her brother's farm in the northern mountains. In scene 4, to secure a roof over their head she agrees to a planned marriage with a dying farmer, Yussup. When the Grand Duke is restored, just over two years after the uprising, Natella employs mercenary soldiers, so-called 'ironshirts', to track down her son, who is the heir to her former husband's estate. Michael is discovered and taken to Nukha where a court trial is scheduled to determine the true mother of the child.

At this point the second story takes over and scene 5 begins. We return to the Easter Sunday of the palace revolt and are introduced to the village clerk, Azdak, who discovers a fugitive in the woods and takes him home to his hut for a meal. When he later discovers the fugitive was none other than the Grand Duke himself, Azdak hands himself over to the Court of Justice in Nukha, in the belief that a new social order has begun and he will receive a proper public trial. However, he is mistaken: one oppressive oligarchy is simply being replaced by another. Arriving at the court, Azdak stumbles upon a scene of chaos. The Judge is hanging dead from a pillar, drunken ironshirts are talking about how they have beaten the rebellious carpet weavers to a pulp, and their new employer, Fat Prince Kazbeki, is hoping they will agree to the election of his nephew as the new Judge. Emboldened by the fact that, with the Grand Duke and Michael still alive, Kazbeki needs their support to maintain his precarious hold on power, the ironshirts mischievously decide to appoint Azdak rather than the nephew. In his new role Azdak proves a carnivalesque Robin Hood figure, taking his travelling court to the people and judging in favour of the poor at the expense of the rich. However, Azdak continues to put his own needs first, forcing bribes from all parties and making some dubious rulings in pursuit of his own survival and pleasure.

When the old regime returns, Azdak fears for his life and unsuccessfully attempts to flee, only then to be reinstalled in scene 6 as Judge by the Grand Duke himself. His next task is to preside over two trials: one is to determine Michael's future and the other is to decide whether an old married couple will be granted the divorce they long for. After hearing Natella on the bonds of blood, her lawyers on the importance of securing the estate, and Grusha on how she has 'brought up the child to be friendly with everyone' and 'taught him to work as well as he could' (88), Azdak institutes the famous chalk circle test: 'The true mother is she who has the strength to pull the child out of the circle, towards herself' (94). Two tests are conducted, and Grusha's refusal to pull Michael for fear he will be torn to pieces convinces Azdak that she is 'the true mother' (Figure 3.2). Instead of signing the divorce papers for the old couple, he annuls the marriage between Grusha and Yussup, freeing Grusha to live with Simon and advising her not to stay in town with Michael. He also legislates that the Abashvili estates be turned into a public playground.

Laying aside the robes that have become too hot for him, Azdak invites all court attendants to a farewell dance, disappearing behind the dancing couples as Arkadi Cheidze sings a brief epilogue:

> But you, who have listened to the story of the Chalk Circle
> Take note of the meaning of the ancient song:
> That what there is shall belong to those who are good for it, thus
> The children to the maternal, that they thrive;
> The carriages to good drivers, that they are driven well;
> And the valley to the waterers, that it shall bear fruit.

(97)

Figure 3.2 The chalk circle test in the 1954 Berliner Ensemble production. Photo by Percy Paukschta, © Inge Steinert, image courtesy of BBA

This song invites us to consider the many relations between the teachings of the frame and those of the inner play. In the opening commune plot, the farmers' decisions validate the idea that land and any other means of production should belong to all and be put to use by those who can best make them serve the common good. Their dialogue demonstrates the workings of an egalitarian legal system, one made possible by new social arrangements, such as collective farms and socialist government, and new forces of production, including agricultural technology and scientific thinking. In medieval Grusinia, by contrast, we see how justice and prosperity for all is made impossible by a private property and class system in which ownership is determined by the ruling elite through their soldiers and law courts. In such circumstances, the Golden Age of Azdak's rule can only be short-lived. However, the subversive actions of Grusinia's kitchen-maid and clerk contribute to the history of resistance and the models of revolutionary practice it can provide. The ruling in favour of the foster mother, who will teach the child friendliness and how to work, rather than the biological mother, who will make sure he 'wears the shoes of gold/ Tramples on the weak and old' (93), constitutes a provocative child-care suggestion both for the kolchos members and the off-stage spectators. Not only the production of wine, law and art, but also the education or (re)production of humans must be changed if we want a fairer world.

A HISTORICIZING EPIC

HISTORICIZATION ON PAGE AND STAGE

In a journal entry of 9 November 1949 Brecht described *The Caucasian Chalk Circle* as one of the 'few real repertoire pieces' by a German author, a play that could be performed at almost any time period because it dealt with general or common themes (Brecht 1993: 423). He does not elaborate, but, as the plot makes clear, the play certainly explores the nature of law and identity and the defence of kin and property, recurrent topics in the history of human culture. However, the label 'repertoire piece' was not meant to imply that his treatment of such issues was valid for all peoples at all times. As the play's genesis, its chalk circle imagery and the staging demonstrate, Brecht's approach to content and form was shaped both by specific historical contexts *and* his desire to respond to them in a historicizing rather than a generalizing manner.

Brecht first used chalk circle imagery in 'The Elephant Calf', a ludicrous interlude in his 1925 version of *Man is Man*. One source for the motherhood test was the Old Testament account of Solomon's threat to resolve a similar dispute by slicing the child in half with a sword (I Kings 3, 16–28). Another source was the adaptation by the contemporary German poet Klabund (Alfred Henschke) of Li Xingdao's thirteenth-century 'Chalk Circle' play. In both Klabund and the Bible it is the biological mother who is judged the true parent. In *Man is Man* Brecht inverts the test and makes the would-be child, Elephant Calf (played by docker Galy Gay transformed into soldier Jeriah Jip), be the one who must pull the mother (played by soldier Uriah) out of the circle. This parodic trail highlights the 'man-made' and fluid nature of identity at a time when Brecht was responding to the upheaval of renewal and intensified modernization after the First World War by celebrating man's transformability in a technologized mass (see Chapter 1).

Brecht redeployed the chalk circle imagery in *The Augsburg Chalk Circle*, a short story he wrote in Denmark in 1940 when in exile from the Nazis. The historical circumstances had thrown up a new issue, man's malleability in the hands of a fascist collective. Now, while the child is reinstated as the object of dispute, the foster mother replaces the biological mother as the true parent. This new inversion can be read in part as a forceful challenge to the Nazis' organization of society around ties of blood and racial purity. Written four years later, *The Caucasian Chalk Circle* continues this challenge. In addition, the 'Prologue' also attacks another cornerstone of Nazi **ideology** – the emphasis on old ties and emotional attachments to territory which were used to justify the expansion of the Third Reich through warfare (White 1978: 163). Written at a time of hope and uncertainty, when Hitler's armies were being vanquished on all fronts, this frame play and the inner play both warn against a divisive post-war settlement and further imperialist territorialism in Europe.

Against imperialism Brecht pits examples of communitarian society and behaviour, situating them symbolically in the Caucasus, the first Soviet territory to be freed from the German invaders. Originally he chose a 1934 pre-war Soviet setting for his 'Prologue', but soon changed the setting for the valley dispute to a badly shelled village in the Republic of Georgia *after* the exodus of Hitler's army. This enabled him to demonstrate both his interest in post-war reconstruction and his vision of how a new communist society could be forged. That vision was both celebratory and critical of the Soviet past. Brecht's admiration for the modernization of agriculture under Soviet communism, and the encouragement of female leadership in the field, led him to depict characters such as the girl tractor driver and the female agronomist who support the irrigation plan, types commonly found in Soviet-inspired **Socialist Realism**. However, the portrayal in the frame play of the resolution of a dispute through humorous negotiation, with minimal intervention from the state's representative, enacts a forceful correction to Stalin's bureaucratic dictatorship with its infamous 'show trials'. A parallel corrective force animates the inner play, which, through its depiction of Azdak's disappointment at the brutal crushing of Grusinia's carpet weavers and the reassertion of an oligarchy, warns against the transformation of revolutionary energy into totalitarian regimes.

The hybrid form of the *Chalk Circle* is attributable not only to Socialist Realist art but also to the American stage and screen of the early 1940s. Initially conceived in part as a vehicle for the Academy Award-winning actress Luise Rainer, who had helped Brecht obtain a Broadway contract for the play before he had written a word of it, the play was influenced both by the need to address an American audience and by Brecht's interest in experimenting with local commercial and popular culture. One aspect that caught his experimental eye was the use of suspense in Chaplin's films and the 'shows' and burlesques of American popular theatre. In his 1944 notes to the play he cited, as a source of inspiration, their use of tension 'focused not merely on the progress of the plot ... but more on the question "How?"'(Brecht 1976: 299). Long wary of dramaturgy that used suspense merely to draw attention to *what* was going to happen next, here he praised the way it was used to generate a consideration of *why* and *how* things happen. This said, Brecht was not averse to using suspense in a conventional fashion. Some episodes in scene 3, particularly Grusha and Michael's narrow escape from the palace soldiers after crossing a frayed rope bridge over a precipice, owe more to the influence of the Hollywood Westerns, gangster films and 'action flicks' that Brecht the movie-buff saw in Los Angeles than to any experimental use of suspense. However, as the musicians make clear at the opening of scene 3, when they sing 'How will the merciful escape the merciless/ The bloodhounds, the trappers?' (25), what is at stake in the scene as a whole is not *whether* Grusha will escape, but *how* in her social context she will manage it.

According to Brecht the play's structure was also conditioned by a negative response to his host culture, particularly a 'revulsion against the commercialized dramaturgy of Broadway' (Brecht 1976: 299). During the play's gestation, Hollywood and Broadway repertoire was characterized by a high percentage of upbeat musicals and escapist comedies, an antidote to the sombre mood produced by nearly three years' involvement in war (Lyon 1999: 242). Often Brecht managed the difficult task of trying to appeal to and re-educate a new target audience, comfortable with art he found repellent, by subversively appropriating commercial forms. Take, for example, the way the *Chalk Circle* plays with the ingredients of a commercial happy ending. Loose ends are neatly tied up, but only through coincidences – such as the timely reinstatement of the Grand Duke and Judge Azdak – that are glaringly artificial. The lovers are reunited, but instead of the boy getting the girl and settling down, the kitchen-maid foster mother gets the noble child, a divorce and a new man, but must soon take flight, for Nukha is once again governed by ruling-class law. A ritualistic dance finale in the play, replaced in the production by a procession *to* the dance, celebrates the triumph of justice and productive nurture. But when Azdak removes his robes and disappears behind the dancers, an air of uncertainty and loss troubles the revelry, an air accentuated in the staging by the notable absence from the procession of not only Azdak, but also Grusha and her family. Is this an unequivocally joyous and closed ending? Was it so for the 1954 GDR audience, which knew that the progressive step towards the Golden Age concretized on stage in scene 1 had yet to be realized off stage?

The Ensemble production was staged at a time when the shadows of both Hitler and Stalin and the start of the Cold War were threatening the advent of a Golden Age. Only a few months before rehearsals began, East German workers had taken to the streets in the strike of June 1953, many of them frustrated with their government's Stalinesque attempt to force the pace of modernization through dictate rather than dialogue (see Chapter 1). In his letters to key political figures at this moment of crisis, and in the *Chalk Circle* production,

Brecht promoted the idea of collaboration, urging government and artists to work together to enhance public discussion about communism and its construction. That Brecht believed theatre should be used to help publicize and rehearse new ways of resolving dispute, distinct from the combative legal proceedings of the Nazis and other imperialists in European history, was particularly evident in the way he directed the actors in the valley scene. Steering them away from their tendency to make the discussion formal, as if in parliament, or wild and tumultuous in the manner of freedom fighters from a heroic Schillerian drama, he suggested they play with dry and light spontaneity. As Bunge noted, the aim was to model unfamiliar behaviour, and to highlight the extraordinary fact that, for these farmers in a semi-mythical socialist society, such behaviour was completely ordinary (Hecht 1966: 80).

The staging of the valley scene demonstrates clearly how Brecht the historicist sought to provoke both a celebratory and a questioning attitude towards the contemporary GDR by comparing it not simply with the past but also with an imagined future society. On the one hand, he reminded the performers that they must take a more historically specific approach to their portrayal of the farmers, criticising their tendency to erase any differences between life at the end of the Second World War and their own experiences in a more prosperous environment nearly a decade later. Partly for this reason he corrected their casual treatment of the moment when the goat-herders present their cheese for inspection, reminding them that in the wake of war such a commodity was a precious rarity. To help build the episode into a historical moment, he swiftly replaced the rehearsal prop they were using – a piece of bread wrapped in paper – with an enormous round cheese, suggesting that it could be carefully unwrapped and distributed to all (BBA 945/34). Brecht's love of cheese was not the only culinary issue at stake here. Performing the cheese offering in this ceremonial way provided the GDR audience with an opportunity to remember the material and social developments in their country since the war. On the other hand, Brecht also asked the performers to create behaviour, such as the way the farmers managed dispute, which was inspired more by a vision of *possible* rather than by actual socialist practice. Through a defamiliarizing comparison with both the past and a potential future, and the use of a setting that mixed actual history with myth, Brecht encouraged reflection on the achievements and shortcomings of his contemporary GDR, a reflection designed to stir all participants in his theatre to action in the present.

EPIC DEMONSTRATION AND DRAMATIC EXPERIENCE

One related defamiliarizing strategy that characterized the staging was an emphasis on *demonstrating* the 'pastness' and artificial nature of the characters and situations being re-enacted. In a more varied manner than any other Ensemble staging, the *Chalk Circle* foregrounded the epic act of telling something about a historical and mythical past (see Chapter 2), and the rehearsed and socially critical nature of that telling. Pieces of business like the cheese ceremony exemplify the more subtle and embedded epic acts in Brecht's theatre. In addition, this production contained numerous overt methods of epic demonstration, such as when the Singer informs the spectators in the frame play that he, his musicians and the host villagers are going to present an ancient tale. The villagers' use of masks, the demonstrational acting, and the Singer's narrative interjections constantly reminded the spectators of the inner play's constructed and partisan nature. The epilogue, addressed directly to both the on- and off-stage audiences, is another overt epic device. Many of Brecht's plays use prologues and epilogues to encourage the spectator to engage with the contemporary relevance of their lessons from the past, a strategy I playfully echo in this chapter.

A further defamiliarizing element in the production was the sustained friction between epic demonstration and dramatic illustration. In dialectical fashion, epic elements were juxtaposed no less overtly with dramatic theatre elements, such as melodramatic scenes that encouraged emotional involvement in the here-and-now of the stage world. In this section I not only introduce you to the multiple modes of demonstration employed in the production, but also illustrate how and why demonstration involved an interplay between the analytic and emotive, between present-tense drama and its interruption through the use of **defamiliarization** techniques.

Like ancient Greek epic poems, the *Chalk Circle* contains episodic tales about national history and legend, and the greater part of its narrative sections are to be performed by a master of recitation and song. The musically accompanied ancient epic was a source of inspiration for Brecht, leading him to request for the production a kind of music which would permit the delivery of a lengthy text. Meeting this request required Dessau to compose forty-eight separate pieces of music, including forty-one songs. However, Brecht's text diverges from its ancient counterpart, particularly in the way it places marginalized voices (such as farmers, clerks and kitchen-maids) centre-stage. Moreover, as Arkadi Cheidze tells the Reconstruction Expert, on this occasion solo recitation is to be replaced by a play with songs performed collaboratively with his fellow musicians, and almost the entire Rosa Luxemburg kolchos, who have been rehearsing under his tutelage.

In the Ensemble staging of this new musical theatre, particular emphasis was given to the fact that the Singer had scripted, and was now orchestrating, the kolchos performance. Positioned alongside the nine singers and instrumentalists, who were seated both on the stage and in a side-box of the Theater am Schiffbauerdamm stage right (on the left-hand side from the audience's point of view), he peered through prominent spectacles at a well-thumbed script with slips of paper in it, thereby drawing attention to the rehearsed nature of the proceedings. His two female co-singers also used books, the act of reading helping to disrupt the illusion of spontaneity. In early rehearsals Brecht and his scenographer sought to shatter this illusion even more forcefully by experimenting with configurations in which the Singer's ensemble performed simultaneously to the kolchos farmers positioned upstage behind them – either live actors or a painted backdrop depicting the kolchos members – and the 1954 spectators before them in the auditorium (Fuegi 1987: 139). This idea was soon abandoned, in part because it required a type of acting that had yet to be developed in Western theatre (Hecht 1966: 97). In the production itself the performers simply played to the auditorium, thereby turning the theatre audience into attentive Caucasian farmers.

Introduced as a Soviet comrade and artist, the Singer repeatedly alerted the audience not only to the fabricated nature of his tale, but also to the fact that it was a Marxist telling. His partisanship was further emphasized by the way his lyrics expressed support for the disenfranchized and a commitment to social change. The casting of Ernst Busch, a star familiar to the German audience as a dedicated communist with a proletarian and activist background, further underlined the politics of the Singer's poetry. Like the ancient Greek chorus, the Singer was also a key contributor to the production's combination of epic and dramatic elements. In addition to announcing entries and exits, he anticipated, commented on and summarized events. These interventions highlighted the action's status as fictional drama, while at the same time encouraging a socially engaged attitude towards the on- and off-stage worlds. The Singer also helped link the actions in each episode and externalized some characters' unspoken thoughts and emotions, helping to create present-tense action. Whether contributing to narration, commentary or drama, the Singer appealed to both the intellectual and emotional faculties of the audience, as well as their senses, encouraging them to adopt a critical attitude similar to his own.

As the Singer's commentary on the downfall of Georgi Abashvili illuminates, this complex appeal was established at the very beginning of the inner play. As the arrested Governor is led away, the Singer not only informs the audience that he will be executed but also comments on the social significance of his death:

> When the houses of the great collapse
> Many little people are slain.
> Those who had no share in the fortunes of the mighty
> Often have a share in their misfortunes. The plunging wain
> Drags the sweating beasts with it into the abyss (16).

This narrative discourages the kinds of emotions that are created by the suspense of not knowing *what* will happen to the Governor or his subjects, and instead encourages reflection on *why* the palace revolution will bring no relief. It also reminds us that feudal ruler Abashvili is a social type scripted by the Singer, one similar to a stock character from medieval drama. However, Cheidze's description of a dehumanizing class structure is emotive, inviting the audience to share his attitudes towards the 'plunging wain' and 'sweating beasts'.

Even in expressive moments such as the lovers' 'reunion' at the end of scene 4, a complex mix of analytical and empathetic responses was sustained. When Simon finds Grusha in the northern mountains after the war, the physical barrier of a stream, Simon's shock at her marriage and motherhood, and Grusha's justified fear that a truthful explanation of Michael's ancestry will be overheard, all combine to bring their ability to communicate to a standstill. In Brecht's staging the two lovers stood silently facing each other across the stylized representation of a stream — two parallel ground-rows of rushes placed on the diagonal – while the Singer narrated what Simon wanted to say about the horrors of war and Grusha about Michael's adoption. According to Hurwicz, Brecht directed the Singer not to narrate Simon's accusatory thoughts in the usual detached manner, but to express anger and reproach (Hecht 1966: 63). At the same time, the actors playing the lovers were to accompany the Singer's lyrics with finely modulated facial movements, expressing attitudes like distrust and disappointment.

This depiction of the lovers' attitudes certainly invited empathetic and sympathetic responses to each individual's situation. Yet the content of their narratives made it clear that social warfare had shaped their situation. Moreover, the presentation of each character simultaneously by two different means – aurally by the Singer and his musicians, and visually by the miming actors – was a reminder that these flesh-and-blood characters were also artistic signs. In this adaptation of techniques from Japanese and Chinese theatre, fruitful tension was generated between responses caused by emotional involvement and present-tense flow and those aroused by analytical commentary and the interruption of a spontaneous here and now. While Brecht's theatre had long been characterized by this tension, it was in the 'Appendices to the Short Organum', written in the same year as the production and influenced by the recent translation of Mao Tse-tung's article 'On Contradiction', that Brecht first clearly articulated his dialectical interest in this complex interplay.

Ernst Busch's doubling of the roles of Singer and Azdak opened up another layer of dialogue between demonstration and experience. While Brecht's text does not specify such casting, a reduction of the Singer's part in Azdak's story, particularly in the final trial scene, makes doubling possible. The Singer becomes less prominent at the moment when the articulate Azdak enters and begins to assume the role of ironic social commentator. That the Ensemble production wanted to connect these characters was indicated not only by the casting but also by the suggestion at an early *Arrangement* rehearsal that the first transformation of the Singer into Azdak should be emphasized by carrying it out in front of the curtain (BBA 944/13). In the opening stages of Azdak's story the Singer continues to make frequent interjections, requiring Busch to make quick and explicit shifts between the two characters and thereby transgress the conventions of illusionism. In scene 6, where the Singer's role is minimal, this sort of transgression was reduced and the present-tense drama progressed with far less interruption. However, though the intensity of the role doubling and sung narrative might have changed, other modes of demonstration were still in force, for scene 6 is a court trial rich in demonstrational features – such as public narration of past events, presentation of argument and evidence, overt social role play and calls for judgement. Not surprisingly, the courtroom trial was one of Brecht's favourite models for epic theatre.

A BERLINER ENSEMBLE SHOW

TELLING THE *FABEL* THROUGH SCENIC WRITING

The way the Singer and his team carried out their storytelling – laying bare the social significance of its events and the social attitudes and interpretative approach of their participants – in many ways echoed Brecht's work during rehearsals. Operating as a playwright-director, he made his starting and finishing point the so-called **Fabel**, the plot of the play 'as retold on stage from a specific point of view' (Kinzer 1991: 27). Here 'plot' is to be understood as a sequence of both interactions between characters and individual **gests**, developed in accordance with a Marxist attention to contradictions. Brecht was particularly keen for the *Fabel* to be communicated through visual means such as scenography and *Arrangement* (the configuration and movements of the actors), often stating that even if the spectators were deaf, or forced to watch through a glass wall blocking the sound, they should be able to follow the *Fabel*. As directorial assistant Carl Weber notes, 'the term "scenic writing" may best convey what Brecht was aiming for' (Weber, in Thomson and Sacks 1994: 181).

Right at the outset on 17 November 1953, Brecht indicated that for him the point of rehearsals was to experiment collaboratively with ways of telling the *Fabel*. His dialectical and analytical approach to the play text was crucial to this experimentation. Brecht encouraged a unique awareness of the text and its staging as a unified whole. While it was common in his day for actors just to have a copy of their own lines and dialogue and to attend rehearsals only where their characters were involved, each Ensemble actor was given the entire text and was encouraged to come to every rehearsal. At the same time, however, by not conducting a read-through rehearsal and not choreographing the play chronologically from scene 1 to scene 6, he disrupted the actors' experience of the text as a sequence of interconnected scenes. Moreover, he often rehearsed a particular episode as a self-contained unit, almost as if the play consisted only of this one segment.

This preference for analytical segmentation and episodic structure ('each scene for itself') also informed Brecht's use of the prompter. He urged his actors to work without the script, receiving each line like he did from the prompter, and then to present it through a full, bodily expression of the character's **comportment**. This sentence-by-sentence procedure was one of many methods that helped create a surprised and questioning attitude towards the development of the action and inhibited actors from being content with prematurely fixed renditions. Others included:

- withholding any overt statement of a directorial concept at the first rehearsal;
- directing by posing questions rather than giving commands;
- resisting actors' requests for run-throughs, the uninterrupted playing of a scene which might make it easier for them to memorize actions and words;
- giving directorial assistants frequent opportunities to test their own suggestions.

By these means, and his 'Who wrote this play?' attitude, Brecht strove for an environment that encouraged dialogue and was open to change.

A key dialogue partner in the telling of the *Fabel* was the scenographer Karl von Appen. Rather than give von Appen a detailed description of how he visualized the production well in advance, Brecht made some brief comments at the beginning of the rehearsal period, and added the hint, 'Cribs, crib figures' (Hecht 1966: 95). Out of this cryptic remark, Brecht and von Appen developed a look for the inner play that was modelled on European nativity scenes and other folk art – particularly that of Brecht's own southern Germany. This aesthetic helped clarify not only *how* the inner play was told but *why* and *from what perspective*. For example, it accentuated the play's secular reworking of events and figures from the Old and New Testaments. If the Grusha story echoes the archetype of the Holy Family, replete with virgin mother, an exalted child, and an official father called

'Yussup' (recalling 'Joseph'), it also secularizes the story by, for instance, *not* making the virgin mother the blood mother and thereby rendering the Holy Spirit superfluous (Nussbaum 1993: 43). And if Azdak is a clown-like Christ figure, journeying through the country with the sacrament of a new Law and being beaten, stripped and almost strung up by soldiers (Suvin 1989: 168), his actions are directed towards social change in the here and now and the establishment of a secular Garden of Eden.

One formal aspect of nativity art adopted by the Ensemble was its non-illusionist artifice and open display of the makers' labour. For example, Brecht sought to reproduce the visibility of the stitched seams in crib-figure costumes, exposing them even further on a stage bathed in bright, cool lighting. The scenography also captured the naive quality as well as the overladen, gaudy splendour of nativity scenes. In scene 2, the palace and church were metonymically repre-sented just by two ornate, door-like facades (Figure 3.3). Made of *papier mâché* covered with copper and silver foil to give the impression of costly, beaten metal, and connected by a curving red carpet, these

Figure 3.3 A version by scenographer Karl von Appen of the ornate, door-like facades and the scene 2 meeting between Prince and Governor. © Volker Schnur, image courtesy of Archiv Darstellende Kunst, Akademie der Künste

facades recalled the inauthentic, mobile and allegorical nature of the crib sets. The Ensemble also adopted the 'stationary' staging techniques employed in medieval theatre. During the 'Flight into the Northern Mountains', as Grusha trudged with Michael on her back against a revolve, the various stations on her journey were represented by simple and easily constructed set pieces that emerged from behind a drop-cloth and travelled towards her. Brecht's allegory, unlike that of nativity and other medieval plays, had a Marxist inflection. For example, the red carpet in scene 2 signposted a direct link between the church and the ruling class. The Marxist perspective was also implicit in a visual code that differentiated characters according to class, the feudal rulers characterized by copper, silver, steel and silk materials, the people by coarse linen. It is important to remember that black-and-white photographs of this and other Brecht productions are a form of documentation that cannot fully capture the allegorical and richly sensuous nature of scenography at the Ensemble.

The production's constant audio-visual reworking of folk, medieval and ancient art not only increased its quotational quality, but also served as an embodiment of the perspective that both dialogue with the past and innovation are crucial to social change. Take, for example, the reference to Chinese art in the white silk drop-cloths against which the action was played – Caucasian mountains in the valley scene, a beehive town of box-like houses for the palace and trial scenes, and gnarled trees, precipices and landscapes to situate scenes set in the northern mountains and to accompany Azdak's travels. Painted in black in the style of Chinese ink drawings, and suspended without battens so that they fluttered like flags, these beautiful backdrops were a reminder of the tale's roots in an ancient Chinese legend. They also functioned as a celebration of contemporary China at a time when the GDR's relationship with the People's Republic was strong, and Brecht was looking to the country as a promising model of how old and new practices could be combined to bring about progressive change (Berg-Pan 1975: 215). The image of the flags' instability and their juxtaposition with the technology of the revolving stage generated a sense of the old art's openness to modification and the value of combining it with modernizing wisdom. The emphasis on cultural dialogue and innovation was also supported by composer Dessau's mixing of folk and modernist art music from Eastern and Western Europe, and his invention of a new instrument called the *Gongspiel*, which combined a set of metal gongs reminiscent of ancient Chinese music with a hammer action and pedals similar to a piano. In echoing the play text's montage of ancient and modern tales and dramaturgy, the production's audio-visual design helped to promote a dialectical perspective towards cultural traditions and heritage.

ORCHESTRATING OPPOSITIONAL *ARRANGEMENTS*

As well as accentuating Brecht's juxtaposition of art forms, von Appen also helped to create the *Arrangements* that clarified the *Fabel*. The two men used a model set with figurines to experiment with composition and choreography, and von Appen also worked independently on numerous *Arrangement* sketches. After the staging had been established, he completed a beautiful series of colour images that vividly convey the lucid and oppositional nature of the Ensemble's *Arrangement*. His image of the episode in scene 2 where the Fat Prince feigns a warm and respectful greeting to the Governor before he enters the church (reproduced here in black and white as Figure 3.3) and production photos of the same moment (see, for example, Hecht 1985: 114), also demonstrates the great extent to which the Ensemble staging was governed by a tableau aesthetic of carefully organized groupings. However, while the model set experiments and sketches provided a crucial springboard for the stage *Arrangements*, they did not set them in stone. After the initial *Stellproben* ('position' rehearsals) for each scene were complete, Brecht turned his attention to individual actions and episodes, altering the *Arrangement* in the light of this work.

Brecht's work on the scene 2 pivot point, which in Bunge's rehearsal notes is given the gestic title 'The Governor's Wife leaves her child behind', illustrates exactly how detailed and experimental his approach was. Considerable time was given to pondering and trying out the different types of gestural complex which could be used to present the abandonment. At a rehearsal in April 1954, Brecht argued that it was relatively unimportant whether Natella fled of her own initiative or was carried away by the Adjutant after fainting, even though this latter behaviour would minimize her responsibility for abandoning Michael, because, for him, the *Fabel* was not a moral tale about the punishment of a bad mother but was designed to show that a child should be kept by the mother who is better for it (BBA 944/98). Three weeks later he suggested that the fainting option was preferable: by placing less emphasis on the guilt of the Governor's Wife, Azdak's decision to award the child to Grusha was made more unexpected and interesting. However, as Bunge disappointedly notes, Brecht again changed his mind, finally opting for the gesture of flight (BBA 945/18–19). An important element of surprise was sacrificed, but Brecht's final choice of gesture not only challenged the notion that female nurturing behaviour is innate, but also extended the criticism of Natella's class-based individualistic behaviour.

As the visual documents and Hurwicz's description of the meeting between the Governor and the Fat Prince clarify, the *Fabel* revealed Brecht's fascination with dynamic, conflict-laden sociological pictures, and his willingness to deviate from his own text in order to establish them. The staging of this meeting lends far greater emphasis than either the text or von Appen's sketch do to the intimate relationship between Natella and Shalva, the Adjutant who later supports her bid to regain Michael and, through him, her right to dispose of her deceased husband's estates. By placing Shalva behind Natella – an arrangement repeated whenever the couple appeared – and by visually linking them in this episode through the suggestive flow of her long train in his direction, the production drew attention to the way the feudal legal apparatus bolstered the ruling class. The inclusion of Kazbeki's Nephew in this scene, and his placement close behind the conspirator uncle, listening attentively to the ambiguous conversation and apeing his uncle's movements, served a similar purpose. In the text the Nephew first appears *after* his uncle has successfully overthrown the Governor and wants to install his young protégé as the new judge. The introduction of the Nephew *before* the downfall not only underlined the nepotism of the aristocracy and its manipulation of the legal apparatus, but also established an opposition between the comfortable incumbents and the would-be usurpers, thereby laying bare the constant state of warfare within the ruling class.

Arrangements such as these show how Brecht used spatial opposition to express social division (Evenden 1986: 136–7). In the scene 4 wedding different types of both spatial and temporal contrast helped convey another social conflict – the division of the sexes through marriage. The most eloquent spatial opposition was that created by the depiction of groom Yussup's farmhouse as two adjoining, but

Figure 3.4 Marriage collides with mourning in scene 4. Yussup's shrouded bed is to the left. Photo by Abraham Pisarek, © Sächsische Landesbibliothek – Staats- und Universitätsbibliothek Dresden

sharply juxtaposed, rooms. The cramped conditions spoke of his family's poverty, and helped explain his mother's desperate decision to marry her dying son in exchange for cash and Grusha's free domestic labour. In addition to this, Brecht used the division to heighten the uneasy mix of wedding and funeral imagery that contributed to the scene's criticism of patriarchal marriage. The contrast between the room on the right – where wedding-cum-funeral guests, musicians and the monk ravenously feasted, made merry and prayed – and the room on the left, where Yussup lay behind a shroud-like curtain, provided an ominous reminder of the marriage's proximity to mourning (Figure 3.4).

This proximity was further highlighted by the staging of the episode's main pivot point, the moment when Yussup, after hearing the guests talk about the war and danger of conscription being over, sits bolt upright in bed and proves he is *not* dying *but* simply feigning illness in order to ensure his survival. Brecht paid great attention to the creation of temporal oppositions through pivot points, interruptive moments at which a scene is given a change of direction and/or a character is given a change of behaviour, using them to create puzzles that could be resolved through social analysis. For example, Yussup's extreme ruse is the product of his social situation as an impoverished farmer who can easily be exploited as cannon fodder. On this occasion Brecht heightened the impact of the pivot point by instructing Hurwicz to bring about an equally shocking opposition in Grusha's comportment. To prepare for it, she was *not* to present Grusha as sad about being treated as a commodity, *but* as confident that the marriage would help her to conceal and support Michael without cutting her off from Simon (BBA 945/78). From the moment of Yussup's 'resurrection', however, her whole attitude was to change. Now the marriage had become a potential entombment, something made even clearer moments later when, in frustration at her unwillingness to scrub his back or give him his other conjugal rights, Yussup reminded her that 'Woman hoes the fields and parts her legs. That's what our almanac says' (56). Through the use of oppositions over space and time the production exposed Grusha's marriage contract as an oppressive economic exchange firmly related to patriarchal property law.

FIXING THE 'NOT-BUT' AND CONTRADICTORY COMPORTMENTS

The staging of this pivot point demonstrates how – and why – Brecht used strategies, such as 'fixing the "not-but"' and juxtaposing comportments, to create each character as an unstable unity of opposites. First, to show that humans are ever-changing entities, constantly shaped by and contributing to the flux of their physical and social environments. And second, to alert attention to contradictory behaviour that is the symptom of an oppressive society in need of change (see Chapter 2). When Hurwicz demonstrated that Grusha was pleased rather than sad about the marriage, she showed that her character had made a decision to adopt a particular attitude and that she could have made it very differently. Her sudden change in comportment clarified how an alteration in social circumstances leads to a marked shift in attitude, and the fact that as a single mother in a feudal – or indeed capitalist – landscape it is difficult for her to make decisions conducive to her happiness. By developing such instances of contradictory behaviour, Brecht underscored what he described in 1954 as the play's main contradictions:

> The more Grusha does to save the child's life, the more she endangers her own; her productivity tends to her own destruction. That is how things are, given the conditions of war, the law as it is, and her isolation and poverty. In the law's eyes the rescuer is a thief. Her poverty is a threat to the child, and the child adds to it. For the child's sake she needs a husband, but she is in danger of losing one on its account.
>
> (Brecht 1976: 304)

His notes and directorial suggestions clarify how he engaged with the *Fabel* in a dialectical way, bringing out 'the contradictions in people and their relationships' and the determinants under which they develop (Brecht, in Rouse 1989: 29).

Brecht's work on the exchange in scene 3, where a peasant farmer charges Grusha an exorbitant price for the milk she must buy for Michael, illuminates how he encouraged a historicizing and dialectical attitude by modelling one himself. According to Bunge's notes, rather than tell the actors what to do, Brecht initially let them play the scene in a conventional way (Hecht 1985: 96). The actors presented an exchange between an essentially or 'naturally' motherly person who is willing to make every sacrifice for her child, and an essentially evil farmer who throws every obstacle in her way. He then provided questions and statements to help the actor playing the farmer observe his character as a historically specific entity, rather than a conglomeration of fixed characteristics. For example, he asked:

- Why does the farmer charge an exorbitant amount?
- Is it because he is a bad character?
- Is the price of milk determined by a person's character?
- Should we doubt that he is capable of being more generous simply because *right now* he is not?

In addition, he suggested why the farmer was being so tough and mistrustful: his hut was on an army road during war and hungry soldiers had stolen goats, his main source of milk. He then asked the actor and Hurwicz to find gests and interactions that would create a contradictory mix of wariness and interested concern towards Grusha, while also hinting at how the peasant might behave if he were in a less hostile world. To this end, Brecht suggested later that when Grusha was struggling to take off her pack, the farmer should lend a helping hand. When the actor expressed concern that this sudden change in behaviour from mistrust to helpfulness was unjustified, Brecht asked why the farmer should have only one side, and pointed out that people are inclined to dispense kindness when it costs them nothing (BBA 945/100). Showing that the farmer was exploitative *and* friendly drew attention to the economic reasons for his contradictory behaviour. And in a more subtle way it also revealed the interpretive activity of the actor and director, reminding the spectator that while we are economically determined we are also capable of changing these determinants.

GESTIC RATHER THAN PSYCHOLOGIZING CHARACTERIZATION

It is evident from the milk-buying episode that Brecht's actors had to adapt to 'a primary concentration on the sociological, behavioral aspects of characterization' (Rouse 1989: 40). Although Brecht acknowledged that there were behavioural elements outside those linked to social class, he believed it was imperative to understand the elements that *were* connected if society was to be changed. While protagonists like Grusha and Azdak displayed multiple attributes, including seemingly 'inborn' characteristics, Brecht focused on the way even these traits were shaped by their social class and circumstances rather than by innate psychological forces. The result was a gestic theatre where rhetorical 'gestures' – the movements, positions and vocal activities of the performer/character's body, as well as gestural extensions such as costumes, props, make-up and masks – externalized the thinking body's socially conditioned relation to time, space and people.

When redrafting the play in 1944, Brecht strove to characterize Grusha as a beast of burden who, by being 'stubborn and not rebellious, submissive and not good, long-suffering and not incorruptible' wears 'the backwardness of her class openly like a badge' (Brecht 1993: 319). His interest in social determination was particularly evident in his treatment of her relationship with Michael. Brecht regarded Grusha's decision to rescue the child as indeed based on certain predispositions, including her tendency to be what he called a 'sucker' (American slang for a person easily fooled), her maternal instinct, and her willingness and ability to be productive (Brecht 1976: 301). However, he also presented these attributes as shaped by the character's role in the mode of production. For example, by contrasting Grusha's activities as a kitchen-maid, used to preparing the Easter Sunday feast, with the utter dependency of the Governor's Wife on her servants when the time comes to pack her trunks, he connected the protagonist's interest and skill in nurturing with her social enculturation. By linking Grusha to the problem-solving agronomist in the valley scene through casting Hurwicz in both roles, Brecht further underscored her social usefulness.

Not only did Brecht present Grusha's behaviour as socially derived, but he repeatedly sought to avoid the presentation of her character as a fixed entity. For example, by foregrounding Grusha's long hesitation before taking the abandoned child he interrupted the idea that her decision was a spontaneous impulse born of an eternally honourable character. In his eyes, the hesitation confirmed her suitability as parent *precisely because* it displayed a class-specific practical bent rather than impulsiveness, a clear-eyed awareness of what might be involved in caring for an infant, with a price on his head, during wartime. His antipathy to essentialist characterization also informed his dialogue with Hurwicz about the depiction of Grusha's bundle during her journey. When Brecht discovered that Hurwicz had been making the bundle smaller and smaller, so as to indicate her character's increasingly pressured economic situation, he commented that such a solution was based on an assumption that it was not in Grusha's nature to steal. His suggestion that perhaps the bundle could become increasingly heavy stemmed from a desire to replace any hint of a fixed noble or 'sucker' character with a subtle reminder of her fluid nature, changed both by circumstances and by her willingness to adopt even anti-social behaviours to survive in an alienating world (Brecht in Fuegi 1987: 157–8). The enlarged bundle also continued the 'beast of burden' imagery, a notion partly inspired by Brueghel's *Dulle Griet* ('Mad Meg' c. 1562), in which a peasant woman, brandishing a sword at the mouth of hell in a chaotic war scene and laden with domestic loot, carries a similar burden. Brecht has stated that any actress who plays Grusha should study the beauty of this painting (Brecht 1976: 299), advice that tells us much about the way he nurtured the actors' understanding of social struggle and ability to express it pictorially.

Brecht's development of Grusha's hesitant comportment and visible burden also helped him to externalize the tension she experiences between her interest in the child and her interest in self, and to identify class-based society as its cause. Grusha's contradiction is only temporarily resolved by the carnivalesque Judge, who himself is troubled by a similar conflict. Described by Brecht as 'a disappointed revolutionary posing as a human wreck, like Shakespeare's wise men who act the fool' (Brecht 1976: 302), Azdak was presented as a type of intellectual who sympathizes with the poor but ultimately puts his own self-interest first. Rather than depict Azdak's 'selfish, amoral, parasitic features' as inborn, Brecht attributed them to his social awareness that the new rulers were simply going to reinstate the old status quo (Brecht 1993: 311). When Azdak first enters the court at Nukha, in chains and dragging the policeman Shauva behind him, his fundamental **Gestus** is that of a defiant man willing to reverse the usual order of things in order to deliver himself up to the judgement of the people. However, once he realizes the golden age of the people's court has not come, he rapidly adopts a *Gestus* of submission, bowing down to the ruling class and its law enforcers in order to save his skin. Throughout the production, Azdak's contradictory comportments not only expressed his fluid and socially determined nature but also his inability, in the given context, to reconcile his interest in serving the oppressed with his own self-preservation and pleasure.

Azdak's self-indulgent attitudes were signposted by means such as the representation of his judge's seat. Brecht arranged for Azdak to be carried by the ironshirts like a sultan in his throne, but suggested that, as his journey progressed, the appearance of the chair should change, becoming increasingly adorned with ornamental altar mats and other precious objects, together with the sausages, ham and wineskins that he had received as bribes or taken at the hearings. As well as expressing his venality, by making the seat into a magnificent processional object Brecht hoped to develop the chair as a witty paradox, a dignified throne being occupied by an undignified judge (BBA 944/72). However, in the chalk-circle trial, Busch presented Azdak not as self serving, but as a revolutionary arbiter for the people who watches the emotional performance of the Governor's Wife, as she tries to persuade him of her rights to the child, with the mistrustful attitude of an experienced trade unionist listening to the 'humane' apologies of the capitalists as they justify a pay cut (Hecht 1966: 85).

The performance of Azdak's appetites also demonstrated Brecht's view of the way in which biological determinants are shaped by class and gender politics. Azdak's transformation of his desire for Ludovica, the voluptuous and well-fed defendant in a rape case, into an exploitative act of conquest is informed both by a class-based desire for revenge and a patriarchal assertion of power (for a more detailed discussion of the way the rape trial was staged, see Chapter 4). Brecht's rehearsal of the scene between Grusha's brother, Lavrenti, and his wife Aniko, who grudgingly offer her shelter during the first winter in the mountains, provided an even more extensive commentary on the way sexual desire and gender relations express or are dominated by economic structures. For example, he insisted that Lavrenti's subservience to Aniko should not be regarded either as the result of innate determinants, such as weakness and cowardliness, or as fundamentally determined by sexual attraction. Instead, its primary cause was her economic superiority as the original owner of their farm and livestock. That he worked hard for Aniko was to be written in the way he conversed, his tired hands resting on his knees rather than gesticulating. In turn, Aniko was to be represented as pleased by and dependent on Lavrenti because of his efficiency as a farmer. Her cultivation of a softly voluptuous image, plus the way she gave him more space at table and the best pieces of meat, guaranteed his dedication and their success as an economic unit (BBA 976/65; 945/73, 87; 944/87).

Brecht's work with socialized gesture in this scene also exemplified his trademark attention to the way a character's thoughts and body were moulded by their role in the mode of production. The function of the play's many soldiers to act as physically powerful and violent defenders of the Establishment's social power and property interests was presented by Brecht as a major source of their crude behaviour and thinking. Thus, he had the ironshirts on guard during the court hearings be depicted as only interested in questions of inheritance and pornographic issues, and as totally lacking in social concern (Hecht 1985: 93). In distinguishing them from other subordinates by giving them full-size masks, like their superiors – with the notable exception of Simon whose masculine beard hinted at his vocational identity (White 1978: 170) – he emphasized both their aspiration to be the masters and a tendency towards the rigid behaviour of men who are trained to take and give orders. Occasionally compared during rehearsal to Hitler's SS, their long, heavy and stiff tabards gave the soldiers a lumbering, tank-like clumsiness, helping to create a fundamental *Gestus* of dull subservience. Here, Brecht's gestic experimentation was clearly tied to his social criticism of the **petite bourgeoisie**, particularly its susceptibility to fascist regimes.

GESTIC MASKS AND STYLIZED NATURALNESS

The masks and costume of the soldiers provided an ideal vehicle for the vivid display of social inscription. They also helped Brecht replace a theatre of psychological realism, oriented around facial expression, with a type of socialist realist performance centred on comportment. As the design and use of the masks in the production make clear, Brecht's realist aesthetic was characterized by the interplay of literal imitation and the playful manipulation of form (see Chapter 2). This interplay reflected not only Brecht's taste for oppositions, but also his belief that, in order to reveal society's causal complex, a realist artist must be concrete and enable abstraction. That is, she must be socio-historically specific, and carefully observe material actuality and the contradictory flux of the real. At the same time, she must be analytical and make legible social causality and the socially significant, i.e. those humans, events and contradictions which are most decisive for the progress of humankind. The artistic means Brecht employed to fulfil this agenda was the combination of literal representation (e.g. the soldiers' behaviour during Azdak's hearings) with defamiliarizing, non-literal representation (e.g. the soldiers' striking tabards). Brecht often described this unity of the diverse as a bringing together of natural-ness and realist stylization.

While the use of masks was a pragmatic solution to the problem of a large-cast play – role-doubling enabling the complex *Fabel* to be told without any loss of clarity – Brecht also ensured that they became a gestic vehicle for displaying socialized comportment. His insistence that the masks should capture the play's multiplicity of social types, rather than blurring them through a fixed schema, such as 'rich people – masks, poor people – none', testifies both to his anti-Formalist position and to his attention to the unity of naturalness and stylization. Not only members of the ruling **class** but also some servants wore masks. Moreover, different degrees of behavioural rigidity were indicated by different sizes, and each mask was individualized and recognizably human. Thus the Governor, the Fat Prince and the soldiers had almost full-sized masks. The Governor's Wife was given only a half-mask in order to ensure that her mouth be kept free for smiling at the Adjutant, a gesture which demonstrated their flirtatious relationship (Figure 3.5). Noticeably smaller and less rigid masks distinguished the professionals, such as the Adjutant, Advocates and Doctors, from

Figure 3.5 Helene Weigel wearing the half-mask of Natella Abashvili. Photo by Thérèse la Prat, © Stadtmuseum Berlin

the rulers to whom they had sold themselves. The palace servants wore small masks, each particularized according to the behaviour of its wearer. A number of characters – the major protagonists, Michael, Simon, Lavrenti and his wife, peasants and many other figures in the northern mountains – remained unmasked. Arguably, even this differentiated mask design erred on the side of the schematic: all those who directly perpetuate a ruling class – masks, all those who do not – none. Nevertheless, the attempt to depict the complexity and flux of the concrete is evident (Mumford 2001: 160–4).

By encouraging a presentational body language in keeping with their stylized nature, the masks also enhanced the demonstrational quality of the acting and the play's nativity scene imagery. At the very first rehearsal Brecht cited the nativity play as the mode of performance he was looking for, later characterizing its acting as similar to the exaggerated and jerky behaviour of circus clowns (BBA 946/31). The masks helped the actors achieve this performance mode by obliging them to use exaggerated gesture. The resulting mime-like style was matched by a forceful vocal delivery, the product of the actors' attempt to match the production's music, which, inspired by music such as folk dance from Azerbaijan and composers like Bartók, was often loud, percussive and full of movement (Fuegi 1987: 148). The simplification and reduction of movements dictated by the masks also helped to isolate and intensify significant comportments. For example, once the actor playing the Fat Prince began rehearsing with his mask it became obvious that his continual fanning movement was not required and that Kazbeki should instead only fan himself at the one moment when he becomes really hot – when the Rider from the capital city arrives, filling him with anxiety that the uprising against the Grand Duke and his governors, and consequently his own plot to murder Abashvili, will be revealed. Here the mask helped to effect the transition from more naturalistic detail to a single, telegraphic piece of business that underlined the power politics of the play.

Even in episodes where there were no characters with masks, such as the one where an exhausted Grusha first sets foot in her brother's home, naturalistic detail was combined with a defamiliarizing demonstration of the socially significant. Scenographic elements, such as the spacious nature of the quarters, the oven, and the sheepskin cover on the table bench, established the relative wealth of the farmhouse. Against its material warmth Brecht carefully built up a frosty social configuration. He set the estrangement process in motion by first transforming the actors' initial agitated manner when playing the episode, one loaded with anger at Grusha's condition, into a more analytical approach by having them add 'the man said', 'the woman said', to the spoken text, thereby helping them to treat their characters as observable objects (Fuegi 1987: 145–6). Slowed by this device, the actors were then in a better position to study the episode's conflictual social relations. The groupings and gestures that ultimately emerged, particularly the uncomfortably sustained separation of Grusha from the couple, made these conflicts graphic. When, for example, a pale Grusha entered the room stage left, supported by a stableman, interrupting Lavrenti and Aniko as they sat sharing a large bowl of soup stage right, rather than rushing to assist his frozen sister obviously on the verge of collapse, Lavrenti remained fixed at his wife's side until her first exit. Such unexpected *Arrangements* and comportments helped to make legible the material and ideological reasons for the couple's unfriendly reception of Grusha. If Aniko is concerned that a relative who seems to be in ill health and a single mother to boot could undermine her financial and social position, Lavrenti is loath to lose his creature comforts by displeasing his wife.

Scenography, props and pieces of business were also governed by a principle of stylized naturalness. Brecht used authentic objects like the sheepskin in the farmhouse, rather than abstractions or symbols, to indicate something about the owner's social context and material circumstances. However, he and von Appen worked in a metonymic way with the set pieces, carefully choosing a few key segments which supplied the outlines of an environment and contributed to the *Fabel*'s commentary. His assistants undertook extensive cultural history research into cultural objects, situations and customs in the Caucasus and medieval Georgia, using their findings when they helped to propel the gist of the *Fabel*. Thus, the Caucasian custom of breaking large, flat loaves of bread by hand was incorporated into the wedding scene, Grusha and her mother-in-law dividing large, flat cakes to feed the starving guests in a secular echo of Christ's miracle with the loaves and fishes. This activity both conveyed the hand-to-mouth nature of their existence and emphasized their need for material rather than spiritual transformation (Fuegi 1987: 147). Both the metonymic use of selected authentic objects and customs and their combination with obviously crafted elements, such as the drop-cloths and masks, provided a reminder that the human world was a constructed entity open to change through the hands and imaginations of men and women.

EPILOGUE: 'THE PROOF OF THE PUDDING IS IN THE EATING'

Animated by a playwright-director dedicated to the progressive reconstruction of theatre and society, the *Chalk Circle* production was both a celebratory and questioning performance, unique in its dialectical unity of the diverse. A testimony to the Brecht collective's mastery of popular and pleasurable entertainment, it achieved success abroad at the International Theatre Festival in Paris in July 1955 and during its tours to London in 1956 and Moscow the following year. The production remained prominent in the Ensemble repertory until the end of 1958, by which time it had been performed about 175 times. But did this richly dialectical pudding actually challenge the culinary tastes and preferences of its historical audiences? And can Brecht's play and staging methods still provide a useful challenge to the way *we* produce and artistically represent our social world?

The initial reception of the production by the East and West German presses, at least until it began to win accolades in Paris, suggests that it had considerable force as an aesthetic and ideological provocation. After the previews in Berlin, the show quickly became contentious in the East, arousing heated cultural debate, yet being pointedly ignored by the Party newspaper. Much of the negative commentary was fuelled by the association of epic theatre with decadent art that deviated from the artistic tenets of Soviet Socialist Realism. Many critics accused the dramaturgy of inappropriately adopting novelistic conventions which jeopardized the play's unity. They referred especially to its lack of a central conflict and resolution, its episodic nature and length, and what were deemed the inadequately established links between the kolchos and chalk circle plots. A key figure in the debates was Fritz Erpenbeck, the editor who five years earlier had turned the Ensemble's *Mother Courage and Her Children* into the first theatre case in the GDR's **Formalism** conflicts (see Chapter 1). Erpenbeck claimed that the artistic unity of the production was also compromised by its failure to reconcile moving dramatic action and realist performance with narrative commentary. For similar reasons he criticised the interiors brought in on the revolve stage in act 3 for being a stylistic break from the more subtly suggestive signs like the palace and church facades and the painted city on the silk drop-cloth. In a fragmentary riposte published posthumously, Brecht defended his experimentation by arguing that the unexpected and unusual were typical and pleasurable components of theatre, and by asking that less attention be paid to the form of his artistic means and more to their social purpose.

Ironically, while the East German arbiters of taste mainly concerned themselves with its formal features, the Western critics focused on its Marxist underpinnings. Scornfully referring to it as a thesis play, they repeatedly singled out the 'Prologue' as a source of tedious didacticism, one commentator describing the valley scene as an attempt to make the entire play more palatable to the East German cultural functionaries (Brecht 1992: 473). In fact, the Party-line Eastern press was also sceptical about the play's overtly didactic elements, though it was concerned more with epic elements such as the masks and narrative commentary. Critics from both sides of Germany also expressed concern about the presentation of motherhood as a social rather than a primarily biological process. The ideological nature of the Western response was particularly illuminated by the controversy surrounding the West German premiere of the play in April 1955 at the Frankfurt Schauspielhaus, a production directed by Harry Buckwitz and overseen by Brecht, with the Ensemble actress Käthe Reichel as Grusha. Angered by what they understood to be Brecht's support for the East German government during the first workers' strike of June 1953, Christian Democratic Union city councillors tried to prevent the premiere. While the production nevertheless went ahead, as a concession to the political environment Brecht authorized the omission of the frame play. Not only did Brecht's art confront the aesthetic preferences of its spectators, but there were also, clearly, occasions when the politics of its audience threatened to overwhelm his art.

Today, after the fall of communism in Europe, Brecht's Soviet setting in the 'Prologue' has become an even more problematic vehicle for his utopian vision of egalitarian law and collective productivity. While in our current landscape of ongoing violent territorialism and intensified battles for material resources, oil in particular, the need for a counter-model has become arguably even more pressing, it may be necessary to follow Brecht's historicist approach and find ways to embody his vision that better suit our particular time and place. One is to create a frame play that foregrounds the relevance of the inner play to a contemporary world. This is the path director Heinz-Uwe Haus pursued in his 1992 University of Delaware production, when he scripted a new scene 1 that depicted the plight of children from the world's trouble spots and their discovery of an old storybook of the Chalk Circle. For those of us interested in the alterable causes of our devastating struggles for land and power, and in ways of better nurturing the future, that story remains both thought provoking and socially relevant.

If it matters to us that productions of *Chalk Circle* are not reduced to hackneyed melodrama about the quirks of fortune, we would do well to learn from the Ensemble's staging. Their pictorial crystallization of class and gender conflict demonstrates how the inner play can be read and presented both as a forceful criticism of the way humans produce and reproduce in class-based societies, and as a celebration of our ability to change invidious habits of ownership. Understanding how the Ensemble approached Grusha and Azdak's stories better equips us to make theatre that questions the large-scale colonization and consumption practices that dominate our landscape, while also modelling a more fruitful stewardship of children and society. Furthermore, the 1954 production shows us how Hollywood-style psychological realism might be supplemented (or even replaced?), and a *Gestus*-based performance developed, in which socialized behaviour is theatrically foregrounded.

The Ensemble's version of gestic theatre was guided by an aesthetic of stylized naturalness, which, in its day, was a revolutionary breakthrough to a more lifelike performance, as Kenneth Tynan's review of their London tour memorably records:

> When the house-lights went up at the end of *The Caucasian Chalk Circle*, the audience looked to me like a serried congress of tailor's dummies. I probably looked the same to them. By contrast with the blinding sincerity of the Berliner Ensemble, we all seemed unreal and stagey. Many of us must have felt cheated. Brecht's actors do not behave like Western actors; they neither bludgeon us with personality nor woo us with charm; they look shockingly like people – real potato-faced people such as one might meet in a bus-queue.

(Tynan 1976: 196)

Brecht's blend of familiarizing imitation and defamiliarizing stylization is a unique political aesthetic. However, in an age when resemblance to everyday reality is the rule rather than the exception in much cultural performance, particularly in the West, we may need to reconsider the use of naturalist imitation. However, any revisions we undertake should be informed by an appreciation of how Brecht and his collective pursued the goal of making the dialectical mode of considering things a pleasure, as they did in model productions like the groundbreaking *Caucasian Chalk Circle* of 1954.

4

PRACTICAL EXERCISES AND WORKSHOP

PREPARING FOR SPECTACTORSHIP

Given Brecht's passionate commitment to changing the way theatre is made and received, his relative silence on the subject of practical exercises is indeed remarkable. While he was a prolific commentator on his aims, preferred models and collaborative stagings, he was far less voluble about aspects of preparatory training such as the nurturing of the performer's expressive skills. Rather than developing a comprehensive system of tasks and activities, like Stanislavsky, or innovative psycho-physical *études*, like Meyerhold, Brecht focused his energies on ways of interpreting and staging the events of the play and their social significance. This emphasis was born both of a tendency to work primarily from the position of a playwright-director and theorist, and of a political interest in telling interventionist stories. Brecht's approach to training is captured in a 1943 journal entry where, in response to a criticism that his productions had hitherto neglected the actor's technique, he remarks that his goal had been to 'base the actor's interestingness on the interest he brings to the social phenomenon with which he is concerned in his acting' (Brecht 1993: 284). Cultivating the actor's ability to generate such an interest was one of Brecht's main contributions to Western theatre. To this end, he encouraged performers to adopt an activist way of looking at society and the stage, and to make this new art of **spectActing** a pleasurable experience for their audience – so pleasurable that the spectators might even take it up themselves!

But exactly how did Brecht prepare the actor and directorial team for the task of being fun and astute commentators on society? By and large, for Brecht the process of actually staging a play was the best way for the actor to develop the skills of an epic practitioner. Rather than devising studio and laboratory sessions in order to create a cohesive way of building a character or new body language, he prepared his actors – who came from traditions as varied as expressionism, realism, agit-prop, cabaret, musical theatre and film – by means of collaborative play rehearsals. However, when faced with the task of addressing student actors, or those unfamiliar with his agenda – including the time in exile in Stockholm in 1940, later in Los Angeles when rehearsing British actor Charles Laughton to play Galileo, or at the Berliner Ensemble in the 1950s, when directing young actors who had come under the influence of Nazi theatre – Brecht did compile a small number of exercise materials. In the first section of this chapter I introduce these *historical* materials and their close relation to the occasional statements on exercises that are dispersed throughout his other writings on theatre.

While Section One below brings the fragments of the past together, Section Two proposes a *contemporary* workshop for Brechtians, which aims to demonstrate that performances concerned with the politics of both **class** and gender may still have something to learn from Brecht. The workshop begins with a series of warm-up and improvisation exercises, and then presents methods adapted from the Berliner Ensemble rehearsals for analysing a text and creating a *Fabel*. Like all Brechtian models, the workshop offers *one* clarifying example of how the training practices typical of Brecht's final years of work can be adapted for a specific twenty-first-century learning context. Brecht's last phase of work is by no means the only exciting or relevant period of practical experimentation in his career, but it is the best documented and, thanks to the Ensemble's acclaimed tours to cultural capitals in Europe, one that had a considerable impact on the next wave of Western theatre innovators.

SECTION ONE: REMEMBERING EXERCISES FROM THE PAST

What appears to have stirred Brecht to write his first, small collection of exercise materials was a desire to assist his actress wife, Helene

Weigel, with her work in Stockholm teaching acting students who had little knowledge of **epic theatre**. The extant materials include 'Rehearsal Scenes for Actors', a series of interlude and parallel pieces to be played in alternation with episodes from texts by Shakespeare and Schiller. Brecht's explanatory notes clarify that the interludes were simply to be inserted between relevant consecutive scenes during rehearsal. How Brecht envisaged the actors' work with the parallel scenes is most clearly mapped out in a journal entry on the Shakespeare studies at the acting school. Here he notes how an attitude of astonishment towards the classic text was generated by a three-phase estrangement process that involved: first, acting a scene from Shakespeare; then playing a parallel 'scene from daily life with the same theatrical element'; then replaying the Shakespeare episode (Brecht 1993: 43). Both the interlude and the parallel scenes function as **V-effects**, providing a lesson in the art of looking at the plot and characters from the classic texts with fresh and socially critical eyes.

A translation of two interlude pieces for *Romeo and Juliet*, and one parallel scene for *Macbeth*, is available in *The Drama Review* (1967: 108–11). The somewhat comic *Romeo and Juliet* interludes, to be inserted just before the balcony scene (Act II, ii), demonstrate how the star-crossed protagonists' self-absorbed pursuit of their own desires jeopardizes the material existence and love lives of their servants and leaseholders. In his introductory commentary, unfortunately not included in the translation, Brecht describes the interlude as a method for helping the actors to build richly contradictory characters, and cautions against treating it as verification of the saying 'one person's pleasure is another person's pain'. In the case of the *Macbeth* episode, Brecht translates Shakespeare's Act II, scene iii into contemporary prose. Shakespeare's scene depicts Macduff's discovery that King Duncan has been slain at Macbeth's castle, and the attempts of ambitious Macbeth and his wife to cover their tracks by framing the King's slumbering chamber men as the culprits. Brecht's scene demonstrates how a Gatekeeper and his Wife, fearful of losing the roof over their heads, attempt to conceal her responsibility for breaking the birthday present for the Lord of the Manor – a Chinese God of Good Luck – by incriminating a sleepy beggar. According to Brecht's commentary, the parallel scene was designed to discourage actors of his day from playing temperamental reactions to events rather than the events themselves, and to encourage them to view the verse speech of the original text as something special and out of the ordinary.

At approximately the same time as he composed the rehearsal scenes, Brecht wrote 'Exercises for Acting Schools'. This terse list of concrete activities is readily available in John Willett's volume *Brecht on Theatre* (*BT*), if a little tucked away in the endnote for 'The Street Scene' essay. Willett's translation reads as follows:

(a)   Conjuring tricks, including attitude of spectators.
(b)   For women: folding and putting away linen. Same for men.
(c)   For men: varying attitudes of smokers. Same for women.
(d)   Cat playing with a hank of thread.
(e)   Exercises in observation.
(f)   Exercises in imitation.
(g)   How to take notes. Noting of gestures, tones of voice.
(h)   Exercises in imagination. Three men throwing dice for their life. One loses. Then: they all lose.
(i)   Dramatizing an epic. Passages from the Bible.*
(k)   For everybody: repeated exercises in production.** Essential to show one's colleagues.
(l)   Exercises in temperament. Situation: two women calmly folding linen. They feign a wild and jealous quarrel for the benefit of their husbands; the husbands are in the next room.
(m)   They come to blows as they fold their linen in silence.
(n)   Game (l) turns serious.
(o)   Quick-change competition. Behind a screen; open.
(p)   Modifying an imitation, simply described so that others can put it into effect.
(q)   Rhythmical (verse-)speaking with tap-dance.
(r)   Eating with outsize knife and fork. Very small knife and fork.
(s)   Dialogue with gramophone: recorded sentences, free answers.
(t)   Search for 'nodal points'.***
(u)   Characterization of a fellow-actor.
(v)   Improvisation of incidents. Running through scenes in the style of a report, no text.
(w)   The street accident. Laying down limits of justifiable imitation.
(x)   Variations: a dog went into the kitchen. [A traditional song]
(y)   Memorizing first impressions of a part (*BT* 129).

* Item 'j' is also missing in the German original.
** Here *Regieübungen* ('exercises in production') could also be translated as 'directing exercises'.
*** Willett translates *Drehpunkt* as 'nodal point', whereas 'pivot point' better conveys Brecht's interest in creating moments of change.

Like shorthand notations written for 'insider' practitioners, these items provide very little information of immediate use to novices. However, when they are cross-referenced with Brecht's other writings on acting and rehearsal, many aspects of the cryptic code can be cracked. In the remaining part of Section One, I discuss those exercises from the list which best illuminate Brecht's performance principles and innovations, using cross referencing to help build a picture of their form and function. Some of the exercises not considered here, such as the search for 'pivot points' (t), are introduced later, in the Section Two workshop.

ATTENTIVE OBSERVATION AND IMITATION

Items (b) through to (g) in particular remind us that Brecht's theatre shared with many other realist traditions, such as Stanislavsky's system, an emphasis on preparing actors to observe and imitate the concrete details of material existence. Although the list tells us little about exactly *what* Brecht wanted actors to imitate, the linen-folding task gives a few clues. Frequently Brecht turned actors' attention to details of social and economic life previously neglected in the theatre, such as work routines, money exchanges and interaction with the tools and materials of production and social life. *How* Brecht wanted actors to approach these details is captured in one of his late theatre poems titled 'Weigel's Props':

> Just as the millet farmer picks out for his trial plot
> The heaviest seeds and the poet
> The exact words for his verse so
> She selects the objects to accompany
> Her characters across the stage. The pewter spoon
> Which Courage sticks
> In the lapel of her Mongolian jacket, the party card
> For warm-hearted Vlassova and the fishing net

For the other, Spanish mother or the bronze bowl
For dust-gathering Antigone. Impossible to confuse
The split bag which the working woman carries
For her son's leaflets, with the money bag
Of the keen tradeswoman. Each item
In her stock is hand picked: … ; all
Selected for age, function and beauty
By the eyes of the knowing
The hands of the bread-baking, net-weaving
Soup-cooking connoisseur.

(Brecht 1979c: 427–8)

What the poem lauds is the discovery of authentic props that both externalize the character's social circumstances and embody the beauty of human productivity. By referencing objects such as Mother Courage's spoon and money bag, Brecht also conjures up images of the way Weigel used props to create social commentary. For example, the oversized spoon hung prominently on an outer garment at heart level, like a strange buttonhole, drew attention to Courage's domestic work as single parent and family provider during the Thirty Years' War. From the moment in the *Fabel* when Courage complains about an 'outbreak' of peace and praises war as better for her canteen, leading the Chaplain to caution her with the old saying 'He hath need of a long spoon who eateth with the Devil' (Brecht 1972: 189), the prop also served as a reminder of the deadliness of trying to feed a family from the big business of war. The spoon's position, in diagonal opposition to the large purse at her hip (used to express pleasure at securing income from canteen deals), helped convey the tragic contradiction between Courage's mothering and mercantile activities (see Figure 2.5, p. 83). What Brecht's praise for Weigel's work with objects suggests is that he was interested in types of observation and imitation that encouraged awareness of the historically specific, economically conditioned and contradictory nature of a character and her social world.

DEFAMILIARIZATION TECHNIQUES AND COMPORTMENT ETUDES

Items such as (q) and (r) remind us that what distinguishes Brecht's theatre from many other realist traditions is its **defamiliarization** of the gestures and texts it so closely observes. In order to disrupt familiar customs and habitual ways of performing, Brecht sometimes used somatic exercises that played with spatial and temporal expectations. For example, eating with over- or undersized cutlery disrupts spatial arrangements and can be used to make strange the social custom of table manners. 'Rhythmical (verse-)speaking while tap-dancing' alters the usual emphases, tempo and line flow of a text, which in turn can generate awareness of the way the text was initially constructed, and of the assumptions underpinning dominant ways of reading it. As Shomit Mitter points out, these temporal dislocations alter the text's meanings and reveal its openness to different readings (Mitter 1992: 55). Brecht used the transcription of verse into the actor's native dialect, and into contemporary prose – as occurs in the 'rehearsal scenes' discussed above – for very similar purposes.

Some of Brecht's experiments with the defamiliarization of text were also designed to help actors artistically crystallize the socially conditioned **comportment** of the speakers, their **gests**. This is the case with exercise (x), which takes as its text the traditional verse poem and song 'A Dog Went into the Kitchen'. Brecht placed the eight-line round together with 'Rehearsal Scenes for Actors' in a collection that he published in 1951 in volume 11 of the *Versuche*, the paperbound volumes intended to introduce his revolutionary experiments. The entire round was also incorporated into the 1953 version of *Drums in the Night*:

> A dog went to (sic) the kitchen
> To get a bone to chew.
> The cook picked up his chopper
> And cut that dog in two.
> The other dogs came running
> To dig that dog a grave
> And set him this inscription
> Upon the stone above:
> A dog went to the kitchen …

(Brecht 1998: 105–6)

According to the explanatory notes in *Versuche*, Brecht intended the round to be recited each time in a new *Gestus*, as if by different characters in different situations. Such an exercise rehearses the type of vocal and gestural precision that is a prerequisite for the vivid externalization of attitudes. The subject matter of the round also provides an opportunity for exploring and illuminating the politics of each speaker's standpoint. For example, the verse could be delivered as an indictment of the needlessly cruel treatment of 'underdogs' or as a vote of support for the cook's position. Alternatively, it could be played as an endorsement of a fatalist 'nothing to be done' outlook, just like that expressed by the *Drums in the Night* protagonist Kragler, who performs the round just as he is deciding whether to support the Spartacists' revolutionary cause or to have another drink of schnapps.

As item (i) confirms, one of the 'classic' texts Brecht used when training actors how to disrupt habitual patterns of delivery and show the *Gestus* was the Bible. Episodes such as the Creation story also proved useful for developing the actor's ability to provide a subversive narrative of prevalent worldviews. Brecht gives an example of this sort of demonstration in the fairground scene from *Life of Galileo*, where he has the half-starved ballad singers present the old Christian view of the universe – a universe dominated by a centrally positioned earth around which lesser objects rotate – as a myth perpetuated by the seventeenth-century clergy who wish to maintain a pope-centred hierarchical society:

> When the Almighty made the universe
> He made the earth and then he made the sun.
> Then round the earth he bade the sun to turn –
> That's in the Bible, Genesis, Chapter One.
> And from that time all creatures here below
> Were in obedient circles meant to go.
> So the circles were all woven:
> Around the greater went the smaller
> Around the pace-setter the crawler
> On earth as it is in heaven.
> Around the popes the cardinals
> Around the cardinals the bishops. ...
> Around the servants the dogs, the chickens, and the beggars.
>
> (Brecht 1986: 82–3)

When Brecht was working with Laughton on the role of Galileo, he used the biblical story to help the actor get beyond the 'familiar, international parsonical tone' which was making it hard for him to orient his speech around the *Gestus*. He had Laughton make a studio recording of multiple first-person narrations of the story. According to Brecht's journal entry of 3 May 1945 – typed entirely in lower case and incorporating phrases written in English, indicated here by italics – Laughton experimented with the following versions:

> a) the creation as recited by a frenchman like jean renoir, b) by a yorkshireman (laughton's home), c) by a cockney (*at the beginning mr smith created the heaven and the earth*), d) by a planter trying to make the natives believe he created the world, e) by a butler (*in the beginning his lordship created …*), f) by a soldier '*in the foxhole*' (with '*so what*' and '*much good did it do us*' between the acts of creation).

> (Brecht 1993: 347–8)

Such an exercise forces the actor to create modes of delivery that lucidly communicate the historical and geographic particulars of the speaker and their (class-based) social bearing. It also introduces one of Brecht's favourite modes of performance: historicizing narration, that is, telling something about a historical or mythical past while simultaneously revealing the bias and historical specificity of the teller's point of view. By adding recording technology into the mix, Brecht effected a further separation of actor from character, giving Laughton the opportunity to analyse the manner of his delivery and its efficacy as commentary on each speaker.

BUILDING THE ACTOR-DEMONSTRATOR

This separation of the actor from character, a process that occurs in all the V-effect and comportment exercises outlined above, is crucial to the development of a seminal figure in Brecht's theatre: the actor-demonstrator who presents and quotes the past actions of another in order to illuminate them in a socially useful way. An initial phase in the building of this figure is the development of a quizzical attitude in the performer towards both characters and sequences of events. To instil this attitude Brecht used rehearsal strategies such as 'Memorizing first impressions of a part' (y), which entails remembering what aspects of the character – on first encounter – seemed strange, surprising, remarkable and contradictory. Brecht proposed a number of other exercises for opening up both a questioning attitude and alternative ways of playing characters, some of which are either described overtly or alluded to in 'Exercises for Acting Schools':

- comparing a woman's portrayal of an attitude or completion of a work task with a man's, see items (b) and (c);
- having each partner take a turn to direct the other by demonstrating their version of the character's actions, possibly one of the tasks suggested at (k);
- imitating the partner and/or that performer's way of playing a character, item (u).

To help actors mark characters and events as historical and separate from the present of the performance, Brecht suggested tasks like 'Running through scenes in the style of a report, no text' (v). Many other quotation strategies are described in the essay 'Short Description of a New Technique of Acting which Produces a Defamiliarization Effect', which Brecht completed in the same period as the list of exercises, and a key writing discussed in detail in Chapter 2.

One method Brecht frequently used to familiarize actors with the actor-demonstrator role was to ask them to imitate models from everyday life. These included: the co-actor or theatre director who, like Brecht, helps the performer to see alternative ways of presenting the character by giving some sketch-like quotations; and the courtroom witness who narrates and re-enacts historical events so that jurors are in a better position to make their deliberations. Item (w) refers to the imitation of a cousin of the court witness, the street-accident bystander who provides evidence for the gathered crowd. Brecht elaborates on the features of the bystander's performance that he wanted the actor to emulate in his 1938 essay 'The Street Scene' (also discussed in Chapter 2). These include the bystander's use of defamiliarizing artistry, such as emphatic, decelerated replays of the victim's actions. He also praises the bystander's ability to take two situations into account: 'He behaves naturally as a demonstrator, and he lets the subject of the demonstration behave naturally too' (*BT* 125). This performer's effortless ability both to show that he is showing, and to combine imitation of the subject with commentary, make him an invaluable model for the Brechtian actor.

SHOWING THE *GESTUS* OF SHOWING

Of all the gests an actor must master, it is the *Gestus* of showing that
Brecht regarded as the most fundamental. This was because he promoted a theatre which openly displays the actor's craft and the constructed nature of the on- and off-stage worlds – unlike fourth-wall
illusionist performance, in which the actor gives the appearance of
having become the character and conceals the tricks used to create
this impression. Brecht's desire to 'enlighten' informs playful exercises
such as 'Conjuring tricks, including attitude of spectators' (a), which
requires the actor to show acts of concealment and the way they place
spectators 'in the dark'. Presenting both conjurer and spectator also
draws attention to the power dynamics involved in the social relation
between the magician-performer and the spectator in his thrall.
'Quick-change competition. Behind a screen; open' (o), which involves
experimentation with the effects of concealed versus open costume
change, offers a moment for a fun-filled comparison of actor–spectator
dynamics in illusionist versus demonstrational theatre.

In his credo 'A Short Organum for the Theatre' (1948), Brecht
explains why he exhorted actors to cultivate the *Gestus* of showing and
lucidly describes an overt method for achieving it:

> This principle – that the actor appears on the stage in a double role, as
> Laughton and as Galileo; that the showman Laughton does not disappear in
> the Galileo whom he is showing; from which this way of acting gets its name
> of 'epic' – comes to mean simply that the tangible, matter-of-fact process is no
> longer hidden behind a veil; that Laughton is actually there, standing on the
> stage and showing us what he imagines Galileo to have been. Of course the
> audience would not forget Laughton if he attempted the full change of per-
> sonality, in that they would admire him for it; but they would in that case miss
> his own opinions and sensations, which would have been completely swal-
> lowed up by the character. He would have taken its opinions and sensations
> and made them his own, so that a single homogeneous pattern would emerge,
> which he would then make ours. In order to prevent this abuse the actor must
> also put some artistry into the act of showing. An illustration may help: we find
> a gesture which expresses one-half of his attitude – that of showing – if we
> make him smoke a cigar and then imagine him laying it down now and again
> in order to show us some further characteristic attitude of the figure in the play.
>
> (*BT* 194)

By playing the cigar smoker – a figure Brecht associated with a relaxed and knowing spectator who was just as ready to exercise his critical faculties in the theatre as in everyday life – Laughton signals his role as spectActor. Brecht's interest in getting actors to adopt the attitude of a reasoning spectator, and to show this calm spectator on stage, partly explains his predilection for exercises which, like item (c), involve displaying the 'varying attitudes of smokers'.

The three-phase 'Exercises in temperament' – items (l), (m) and (n) – testify that creating a *Gestus* of showing often involved more complex opposition, separation and dislocation techniques. In (l) the actors oppose the wives' 'authentic', calm, linen-folding task with the feigned 'wild and jealous quarrel for the benefit of their husbands'. Here, the act of showing the argument is a fake is achieved by having the actors simultaneously carry out fourth-wall imitation (the folding) and verbal playful demonstration or pretence (the quarrel), and by separating gesture from speech. In (m) the imitation of 'calm linen-folding' of (l) is transformed into a silent episode of folding which expresses the women's escalation into conflict. This pantomimic exercise requires the actors to practise externalization of emotion, which in turn 'showcases' their gestural skills. Here the actors also experience inversion of the former physical patterns: they no longer fold calmly, but in an agitated manner, no longer feign a quarrel, but are silent. At stage (n) the quarrel game in (l) becomes serious. Through this three-phase sequence the actors rehearse both the showing of comportment and the juggling of alternative modes of representation (illusion and self-reflexive demonstration). The sequence outlines the diverse techniques – separation of speech and gesture, physical inversion, pantomimic display, and simultaneity of imitation and presentation – that the Brechtian actor can use to challenge habits of performance that often conceal the workings of both stage and social life.

SECTION TWO: A WORKSHOP FOR BRECHTIANS

The following workshop is an adaptation of the historical exercises described in the first part of this chapter, and of the strategies Brecht used during rehearsals at the Berliner Ensemble (see Chapter 3). It is also the product of collaboration with Madeleine Blackwell, a professional practitioner with extensive experience in projects inspired by Brecht's work. She has conducted Theatre in Education and Community Theatre programmes in Australia, and also collectively devised productions in the Asia–Pacific region and South America organized by political theatre scholar-practitioner Eugene van Erven. Together, Madeleine and I have been translating Brecht's practices, those from the 1940s and 1950s in particular, to meet the needs of our students at the University of New South Wales, Sydney. Drawing on that collaborative work, I have devised a programme of exercises for a group of ten to forty members that can be tailored to suit one intensive or two more leisurely three-hour workshops. Part 1 focuses on Brecht's concept of comportment as well as situation scenarios, while Part 2 focuses on methods for rehearsing a Brecht text.

The programme unfolds the application of Brecht's key performance principles in a manner informed by his emphasis on the socio-historical specificity of the participants. For example, many of the exercise scenarios address the reality of early twenty-first-century, middle-class and female-dominated student cohorts who are being trained in an Anglo-American context. The workshop also aims to challenge the common assumption, held by many of these students, that Brecht's theatre is relevant only to practitioners interested in public and class politics. It seeks to do so through demonstrating how his approach can illuminate the socially constructed nature of individual personal experience, as well as the politics of gender. If you are working with a different group profile in another place and time, you will need to apply Brecht's historicizing eye and modify the exercises to meet the politics of your situation.

SETTING UP THE SPACE FOR SPECTACTING

Arrange the workshop venue so that it establishes an environment in which Brecht's interest in spectatorship and picture-making can be foregrounded. For example, a configuration like a thrust stage, created by placing a full row of chairs on one side of a room and a half-row of chairs on each of the two remaining parallel sides, can make the presence and activity of spectators obvious without compromising their ability to see the pictorial gestures and tableaux of the performers. Both the spatial arrangement and the sequence of events should encourage a dialogic environment – in which all participants can move constantly between being active observers who take notes, interpret and make suggestions, and being reflective performers. Those who wish only to observe can be given the role of dramaturgical assistants who carefully record the process. While the running of the workshop requires experienced leadership, the principle of dialogue can be kept alive by having two or more leaders take turns to observe or coordinate, and/or by maintaining a forum atmosphere similar to that fostered by Brecht during rehearsals (see Chapter 1).

CHOOSING THE CLOTHES

In keeping with Brecht's own approach to performance, the workshop is designed to prepare participants to observe and critically depict everyday social behaviour. While studio sessions that introduce the work of practitioners like Meyerhold, Lecoq or Grotowski are likely to emphasize the development of a new physical language through strenuous and sustained training, this workshop emphasizes a Marxist-inspired way of receiving and estranging 'old' social behaviours through a series of 'ordinary' comportment *études* and situation scenarios. Hence, no special clothing is required: it is better for you to be in your usual, everyday clothes.

PART 1

Warm-up 1: strutting your stuff: making familiar bearings strange

This warm-up exercise introduces Brecht's focus on the socialized body.

Every participant walks in the playing space as if they are themselves in a familiar social circumstance specified by a workshop leader (WL). In the case of students, for example, every one could walk *as they usually do when heading to a class at university or college.*

Once the walking is established, the WL asks participants to observe physical features such as:

Gait: what is the nature of your tempo and rhythms? Do you bounce, glide, or march? Do you walk quickly, slowly, lightly, firmly?

Posture: how do you hold yourself? Are you upright or on a slight lean? Is your head tucked into your shoulders or jutting forwards? Is your weight centred in your heels, pelvis and/or chin? Are your fingers curled or loose? How do your limbs and gaze extend into the space?

The WL then asks the participants to increasingly exaggerate the trademark physical features of their walk, using a scale of 1–10 with the WL giving the count. After reaching 10 the WL calls for a freeze. She then selects a number of the walkers and the rest return to the seats. The selected members resume walking, this time at level 5, with each spectator choosing one walker whom they will observe closely.

During the walking, the WL asks the *walkers* to think about whether any aspect of their gait and posture has been shaped by social forces and roles. These forces could include the family, school, church, nation, urban or rural environment, ethnic group, economic class, workplace, sport or art or fashion culture, gender and generation training, or affiliation with other social groups. No changes to the walk should be made at this point.

The WL then asks the *spectators* to analyse their chosen walker's social bearing or comportment. That is, their physical relation *and* attitude to time, space and people. To this end, they should use the following questions as springboards:

1 What is this body's relation to space and time? What is the speed of movement? How much space does it take up? Is it expansive, strident and forceful, and/or meandering and indecisive?
2 What is the nature of its gaze? Where and how are the eyes looking? Fixed and out to the horizon and/or downturned and constantly moving?
3 How does this body relate to the social world? How does it behave towards other bodies in the space? Is it open, closed and/or ambivalent towards others? Is it playful and/or defensive, threateningly confident and/or submissive, pliable or provocative?

When sufficient time has elapsed the WL asks the walkers to stop and form a group with their observer(s) to discuss the issues raised by the three questions, and the social causes of the behaviour. Each group now modifies the walk, including the level of defamiliarizing selection and exaggeration, so that some of these causes are better illuminated. For example, if an older workshop member realizes that on campus she has developed a veiled gaze and pacy, purposeful gait as an act of resistance against being framed as vulnerable and insufficient, modifications such as an increased softening of the gaze (one that neither invites penetration nor reveals a state of mind) and a lengthening of the spine (to maintain upright posture and an impression of capability) might help convey why and how this comportment has been constructed to deflect the gaze of others. Once the modifications are complete, the walkers return to the floor and 'strut their stuff'. The WL calls for a freeze, bringing the exercise to a close with a tableau.

Commentary: While physiology influences many aspects of our body language, Brecht's theatre is interested in illuminating the multiple ways bodies are moulded by alterable socio-economic forces, including the various social groups we participate in or are governed by, and our roles and relations in the dominant mode of production. The exercise above aims to generate a type of Brechtian V-effect, encouraging us to look afresh at social construction processes that are often concealed, taken for granted and/or unquestioningly repeated. It also introduces Brecht's interest in comportment – a thinking body's socially conditioned relation to time, space and people – and in defamiliarizing our social bearing through artistic means such as the selection and heightening of gestures. In addition, by providing an opportunity to air the observers' interpretations of these walks, it highlights Brecht's interest in reception and gives actors an opportunity to reflect on how they can create clarifying gestures for spectators who share some of the performers' values and assumptions, and have divergent ways of looking at the world. What distinguishes this walking exercise from those found in other types of actor and performance training is its Brechtian emphasis on building a **Gestus**, a strikingly vivid and illuminating demonstration of comportment.

Warm-up 2: completing the census: thinking about social class

If the previous exercise highlighted the social construction of our everyday comportment, this second and final warm-up exercise draws attention to social class affiliations and divisions and the fact that these are often concealed. In asking participants to form line-up and cluster formations in response to instructions inspired by social policy documents like the National Census, it also offers a gentle reminder of some of the hierarchies, inequities or opposi-tions that continue to inform our social life in so-called free and fair societies.

The WL starts the game by dividing the group in half and creating two parallel lines. Each line must then try to be first to complete the line-up orders specified by the WL. The initial line-ups should establish a playfully competitive team game with the air of a children's party. As the exercise progresses, and the instruc-tions become more complex and potentially confrontational, it is important to maintain an engaging, fun-filled atmosphere. The specifications for the initial line-ups should be straightforward. For example:

(a) Height, tallest at one end, shortest at the other.
(b) Age – if there are a number of people in the same age bracket, they should compare their birth dates.

The WL then explains that the line-up formation is going to be replaced by more complex cluster groupings. She also indicates which row of chairs people should sit in if they are (a) 'Abstainers' who *do not wish* to place themselves in a group, or (b) 'Motley Crew', people who *cannot* place themselves because they do not believe they belong to any of the categories. People who belong to two or more groups must decide which one, for the purpose of this exercise, they are going to join.

The game continues with participants grouping themselves accord-ing to criteria such as:

(c) Gender, as recorded on their birth certificate or passport.
(d) Current place of residence, i.e. specific suburb or town.

(e) Their maternal grandmother's country of birth.

(f) Religious preference (including atheist and agnostic).

Finally, the WL develops the game into line-ups on a diagonal in the space according to:

(g) Father's annual income from paid work.

(h) Mother's annual income from paid work.

(i) Preferred political party at national level, using a right- to left-wing continuum.

(j) The number of times you have suffered a broken heart.

Commentary: In Anglo-American contexts, where the idea of the self-made man is pervasive, this game serves to remind us of the formative and extensive nature of our social relations, as well as provide visceral experience of how the subject matter of Brechtian theatre continues to be relevant and moving. Some of the formations are light-hearted and designed to generate pleasurable teamwork, while others ask participants to think seriously about their socio-economic positions and whether they wish to declare them publicly. After the game it can be illuminating to consider: the moments when the numbers of Abstainers and Motley Crew increased; the reasons why at certain points it became harder to make a decision about affiliation and its exposure; and whether in another time or place the decision-making dynamics would be different.

Exercise 1: cross-cast interview: creating V-effects

Having set the scene for a concentration on the sociological aspects of individual and group behaviour, the workshop now begins to apply this focus to the building of personae and, from Exercise 2 onwards, characters. In Exercise 1 an interview scenario involving a male interviewer and a female applicant is used as a springboard to introduce V-effects, artistic strategies for defamiliarizing acculturated gestures.

This exercise works best if it can be carried out by one female and one male. It is also preferable if the performers have been involved recently in an interview themselves and have skills in improvisation and imitation. The performers' task is to play a version of themselves in a hypothetical interview and decide quietly together the details of that situation, e.g. where, when and why it takes place. It is helpful if the couple's brief improvisations are recorded on video and played back on a screen large enough for the entire group to see. The performers should use a short series of actions as the basis of the improvisation, such as the following:

> The interviewer is seated at a table facing the audience. There is a knock at a door. He calls out and the interviewee enters. He rises, shakes her hand and ushers her to a seat. The first question begins.

The following versions of the scenario are then played out (if the recording technology is unavailable, the number of versions will need to be adjusted slightly):

Version 1: The performers play their designated roles 'as if' they are themselves in a real interview. The WL stops the interview as soon as the first question has been asked. We already have enough material to work with. The improvisation is recorded on video.

Version 2: A re-play of Version 1, except this time the performers swap roles, the male copying what the female applicant did, and the female copying the male interviewer. To prepare the performers, the WL shows the recording of Version 1. When it comes to the cross-cast version, it is crucial that careful imitation of the partner is emphasized and that parodic or ham acting is avoided.

Version 3: A replay of the cross-cast Version 2. This time the actors consolidate their work, taking into consideration audience suggestions about the accuracy of their mimicry. This version is also recorded.

Version 4: The actors return to the designated roles they were playing in Version 1, but this time each imitate their partner's performance of the role, using the video recording of Version 3 as an *aide-mémoire*. For example, the female performer might incorporate aspects of how he attempted to copy her leg placement as she sat down, which might include a slight pause before and after the placement due to his need to think about how to get the right look.

After Versions 2 and 4 it is important that the audience discuss which aspects of behaviour were made strange by the cross-casting and copying, and exactly how estrangement was brought about.

Commentary: Using gender and workforce roles and relations as its social content, and Brecht's interest in cross-casting as rehearsal strategy, this improvisation makes clear that a fusion of close observation and critical detachment is fundamental to the achievement of a Brechtian V-effect. It also provides an entertaining reminder that many of our ways of behaving and viewing are socialized and habitual rather than natural and eternal. Very importantly, cross-casting can assist performers to develop a questioning attitude towards the familiar. For example, witnessing a male trying to copy the way (many a) female interviewee dips her head a little to the side in a non-antagonistic and arguably submissive way, can make the female performer aware that her/the interviewee's behaviour is learned and only one of many possible modes of operation. She is then in a better position to stage her own questioning of the interviewee's submissiveness by applying another defamiliarizing strategy that Brecht called 'fixing the "not-but"' (see Chapter 2). That is, by slightly exaggerating the interviewee's comportment, or performing it in an awkward manner – and the male performer will give her some ideas about how to do this – the female performer can show, first, that the interviewee is *not* looking at the interviewer straight on, *but* dipping her head, and second, that she is critical of this compliant gesture and its social origins. Such acting allows the necessity and possibility of alternative actions to be suggested.

Exercise 2: taxi ride: showing social circumstances

As Brecht declared during his work in the mid-1950s, Constantin Stanislavsky's idea about researching and fleshing out a character's 'given circumstances' is a method that can be usefully adapted for a theatre interested in creating characters from a socially informed perspective. While Stanislavsky encourages actors to gather all the information relevant to their character provided by the play text and its key interpreters (director, scenographer, actor etc.), Brecht urges theatre makers to view that information with an eye to socially significant gestures and contradictions. The following improvisation task gives performers and spectators another opportunity to view a character as the product of changeable rather than eternally given circumstances.

The successful completion of this task requires a small group of keen actors who will play the roles of Taxi Driver and Passengers, and work with the following scenario:

> A Taxi Driver is parked at the central railway station of a large metropolis at 3 p.m. In turn, three different Passengers, each travelling alone, hail the taxi and start a journey to the city's main airport. Each time, through a series of actions and gestures, body language and small talk, information about the social background and class memberships of both Driver and Passenger is gradually revealed. The set actions are:
>
> 1 Passenger signals to taxi and gives directions.
> 2 Passenger enters taxi with luggage.
> 3 A conversation occurs, one that doesn't give the game away in the first few seconds!
> 4 When the Driver knows enough about the social identity of each Passenger, s/he calls out 'Stop' and then asks: 'Are you … ?' The Passenger replies 'Yes', 'No', or 'Close'. If the Driver is unable to identify the Passenger's social class and circumstances (gender, ethnicity, family background, type of work etc.) s/he should ask the spectators to put forward their suggestions.
>
> *Physical Setup*: Four chairs, two in the front and two in the back, can indicate the car. The WL needs to supply a diverse collection of travel bags, from which each actor will select one or two items that they can use to highlight their Passenger's social circumstances.

Actors can devise their own Passenger character, or be given one from a list such as the following:

(a) Female French teacher at a state secondary school, 42, single, travelling to see French theatre company at a festival.
(b) Single mother receiving welfare benefits, 25, travelling with two (imaginary rather than enacted) children under 4, living in a country town, and going to elder brother's funeral.

(c) Established private-practice cardiologist, male or female, 52, travelling to annual cardiology conference.

(d) Young male bricklayer, going to sister's wedding.

NB: Cross-casting is a defamiliarizing strategy that can be usefully added to this improvisation. For example, the cardiologist can be a female played by a female in one scenario, then a male played by a different female in another. To avoid confusing the spectators and to maintain their attentiveness, the WL needs to announce that cross-casting will be used and to explain that only the Taxi Driver performer will be told exactly which actors are cross-cast and in what way, i.e. cross-gender, cross-race, cross-generation and so on.

The Taxi Driver actor must be a skilled communicator who is able to gather information about each Passenger without becoming imposing, and demonstrate the Driver's attitude towards the different Passengers. Those actors playing Passengers must choose a work or travel bag from the WL's collection. They should treat the bag as a gestic (i.e. *Gestus*-oriented) prop, using the way they carry it, where they place it in the cab and so on to vividly illuminate something about their character's social roles and comportment. They also need to think carefully about where and how their character will sit in the car. All performers must play 'as if' they are the character, trying to avoid clichés and crude stereotypes by carefully observing the character's social circumstances.

Commentary: The type of socialist realism Brecht was interested in combines close observation and imitation of the concrete social world with defamiliarizing abstraction and stylization (see Chapter 2). This exercise encourages theatre makers to move beyond schematic or one-dimensional caricatures and to rehearse the imitation of complex social behaviour, while at the same time selecting vivid comportments that preserve the 'full substance of a human gesture even though it now represents a copy' (*BT* 138). In so doing, the exercise develops an analytical actor who knows what types of Stanislavskian research can be useful, and how to select and use gestures, spatial relations and props to externalize socialization in inventive and persuasive ways.

When the exercise is being carried out, actors often consciously or inadvertently start 'fixing the "not-but"', or presenting socially significant contradictions, and this is something the WL can draw attention to. For example, in a performance of a scenario involving a single-mother character hailing a taxi at the central railway station in Sydney, I noticed the development of a 'not-but' moment at the point when the Taxi Driver asked the passenger where 'she' wanted to go. Obviously distracted by the juggling of bags and children, she blurted out her ultimate destination, 'Melbourne', a city over 800km away from Sydney. This instruction, together with the driver's comment 'Ah, Mascot, domestic terminal', helped to demonstrate that she was *not* a regular commuter *but* an inexperienced traveller whose mobility was restricted by her social circumstances. And in a cross-cast performance of a male cardiologist Passenger, I have seen the female actor develop significant contradictory behaviour by showing 'him' *assertively* asking the driver to stop so he can get out and buy a packet of cigarettes, and then *obligingly* putting the cigarette away when the taxi driver requests that he not smoke in the cab. Through this carefully observed shift from assertion to compliance, the actors helped build up the contradiction of the cardiologist who smokes, a tension that could be used to help direct spectators to ask: why is there so much ill-health in the health profession, and can the industry be cured?

Exercise 3: greetings and farewells: imitating and framing customs

Taking simple greeting and farewell rituals as its social content, this improvisation offers another opportunity to rehearse the combination of imitation and defamiliarization. It also extends the workshop's introduction of the dialectic between empathetic and demonstrational performance that marks Brecht's realist theatre, a dialectic he repeatedly sought to clarify in later writings such as 'Notes on Stanislavski' (1953):

> As a writer I need an actor who can completely empathize and absolutely transform himself into the character. This, indeed, is what Stanislavski holds to be the first goal of his System. But at the same time and before all else I need an actor who can stand away from his character and criticize it as a representative of society.

(Brecht 1964: 166)

This dialectic is created when the actor both plays 'as if' she is the character and from its perspective, *as well as* demonstrating the character's interactions from a problem-solving or change-seeking perspective. A further goal of this exercise is to start the process of learning how to create interruptive pictorial gestures and tableaux.

Phase I: imitation

Participants divide into groups of two to three members, with each group selecting *one* of the following scenarios, which they then act out using a few carefully chosen lines and gestures:

(a) A divider between two contestants slides back on a television dating show and twenty-something XY meets twenty-something XX. They embrace and the compère asks which of them is going to choose the card with their holiday destination.

(b) The newly appointed CEO of a water company from a branch in an English-language country, which has recently failed in its bid to head a local desalination project, meets the CEO of the Tokyo head branch at the Japanese office. They bow and/or shake hands in the latter's office and then sit down.

(c) The American President and his wife bid farewell to delegates and media after a visit to a destitute American city, still in ruins one year after a hurricane. They then wave and turn to enter their private jet back to Washington.

The members in each group should play from the perspective of their character, taking care to imagine and observe social circumstances. For example, those who have chosen the dating show might imagine the following circumstances:

(1) A 21-year-old male economics/law student at a prestigious university with an urban private boys' school background who wants to go into commercial law; his father is a barrister and his mother is a legal secretary in the same firm.

(2) A 23-year-old female honours theatre student at a less prestigious institution, schooled at a rural equal-access high school; her mother is a physiotherapist and her father is a secondary school teacher.

Once circumstances such as social class and training have been established, the actors need to consider how these have influenced the characters' beliefs, feelings and attitudes. The result should be a living sociological portrait, not a clichéd stereotype.

Once all the groups have had time to rehearse their sketches it is important that a small number – preferably each working with a different scenario – show their work in progress.

Phase II: social commentary

All groups now approach their scene from the perspective of a social commentator; that is, they should make the familiar performance of the custom strange in such a way that the audience learns something about the characters' attitudes towards each other and their situation, as well as about the culture the custom belongs to. The commentary will be conveyed both by direct address to the audience and by choices about comportment, groupings and so forth. Issues that could be considered include:

(a) Men's and women's roles and relations in the depicted society.
(b) The behaviour and interrelations of international businessmen.
(c) The relationship between the American President and the media.

The commentary version of the scene should incorporate at least one of the following three elements:

1. Some use of spoken past-tense stage directions and delivery in the third person to describe the characters' social behaviour and attitudes. For example, the performer playing the President's wife might preface one of the character's gestures by saying directly to the audience: 'She stepped back slightly behind her husband, showing the public that she was *not* a meddling *but* a supportive First Lady and that he, the elected leader, was in command.'
2. A pivot point where the power relations change in some socially significant way. For example, in the dating show, a pivot point could occur during the choosing of the card with the holiday destination; or in the case of the water-company CEOs it might take place at the point when a solution is found to the problem of how each should greet the other.

3. Evidence of attention to the contradictory and changeable nature of behaviour and power relations. For example, the hypothetical female theatre student outlined above might be *intimidated* by the confidence and self-presentation skills of the lawyer at one moment, and then *supercilious* when, as they decide who is to select the holiday card, he patronizingly insists, 'Ladies first'.

Once the broad outlines of the commentary are established, the groups need to select the most cunningly simple and vivid gestures. They also need to make sure that the sketch is framed by clear opening and closing tableaux.

The same groups who showed their Phase I work in progress should now present Phase II, with all participants considering what has changed and why.

Phase III: empathy plus demonstration

Sometimes the commentary version can result in a parodic performance where the complexity of the characters is greatly reduced. While Brecht certainly used one-dimensional satirical parody, particularly when criticising characters who perpetuated rather than challenged oppressive habitual behaviours, it was more common for him to present characters – including the objects of his parody – as contradictory entities capable of change. In this third and final version, each group combines social criticism with playing from the character's perspective. The spoken stage directions are excised, their commentary embedded instead in the performers' actions. The episode is repeated until it gives the impression of a polished piece of artistry. To conclude this exercise, groups using the same scenario are combined. The resulting three scenario teams present their work in quick succession, starting with the dating show and ending with the President's farewell. The WL can use a drumbeat or other framing device to indicate the closing of one sketch and beginning of another.

Commentary: Brecht's actors both imitated their characters' attitudes and behaviours, and showed that they were showing these characters from a particular perspective. This exercise introduces the complex vision required of the Brechtian performer, as well as the high levels of artistry involved in selecting the contradictory gestures and tableaux that help present characters and our social world as open to analysis and intervention (see Chapter 2). It also exemplifies how demonstration of the socially significant can be achieved by means of a wide range of performance modes, from comic parody to realism, and how it often involves a rich synthesis of illusionist and non-illusionist acting.

PART 2

The rape trial: arranging the *Fabel*

Part 2 introduces methods for achieving a Brechtian interpretation and staging of the rape trial episode in *The Caucasian Chalk Circle*. It contains sufficient material for at least a two-hour event and ideally would take place after a rest period, preferably in an all-day workshop. However, it can also be abbreviated to form the finale of a shorter event. Its aim is to explore aspects of Brecht's innovative approach to text, especially the way he and his collaborators created the *Fabel*, the plot of the play script as retold on stage from a particular perspective. Here 'plot' can be understood as a series of contradictory character gests and interactions (see Chapter 3). This exercise adapts features of the Berliner Ensemble's rehearsal process for their 1954 *Chalk Circle*. It also reworks rehearsal strategies demonstrated at the Symposium 2000 on Brecht/Directing/Acting hosted by Rose Bruford College, UK, particularly those presented by Manfred Wekwerth, assistant director for Brecht's *Chalk Circle* and Artistic Director of the Berliner Ensemble from 1977 to 1992.

In advance of the workshop, the WL should prepare for this exercise by reading both *The Caucasian Chalk Circle* and Chapter 3 of this book. Participants should read the play and/or the plot summary provided in Chapter 3. They will also need a copy of the following excerpt from scene 5:

> Enter Azdak from the caravansary on the highway, followed by the old, bearded innkeeper. The Judge's seat is carried by a manservant and Shauva. An Ironshirt with a banner takes up position.

AZDAK: Put it here. Then at least we can get some air and a little breeze from the lemon grove over there. It's good for Justice to do it in the open. The wind blows her skirts up and you can see what's underneath. Shauva, we have eaten too much. These rounds of inspection are very exhausting. *To the inn-keeper:* So it's about your daughter-in-law?

THE INNKEEPER: Your Worship, it's about the family honour. I wish to bring an action on behalf of my son, who's gone on business across the mountain. This is the offending stableman, and here's my unfortunate daughter-in-law. *Enter the daughter-in-law, a voluptuous wench. She is veiled.*

AZDAK *sitting down:* I receive. *Sighing, the innkeeper hands him some money.* Good. Now the formalities are disposed of. This is a case of rape?

THE INNKEEPER: Your Worship, I surprised this rascal in the stable in the act of laying our Ludovica in the straw.

AZDAK: Quite right, the stable. Beautiful horses. I particularly like the little roan.

THE INNKEEPER: The first thing I did of course was to berate Ludovica on behalf of my son.

AZDAK *seriously:* I said I liked the little roan.

THE INNKEEPER *coldly:* Really? – Ludovica admitted that the stableman took her against her will.

AZDAK: Take off your veil, Ludovica. *She does so.* Ludovica, you please the Court. Tell us how it happened.

LUDOVICA *as though well rehearsed:* When I entered the stable to look at the new foal, the stableman said to me of his own accord: 'It's hot today' and laid his hand on my left breast. I said to him: 'Don't do that!' But he continued to handle me indecently, which provoked my anger. Before I realized his sinful intentions, he became intimate with me. It had already happened when my father-in-law entered and accidentally trod on me.

THE INNKEEPER *explaining:* On behalf of my son.

AZDAK *to the stableman:* Do you admit that you started it?

THE STABLEMAN: Yes.

AZDAK: Ludovica, do you like to eat sweet things?

LUDOVICA: Yes, sunflower seeds.

AZDAK: Do you like sitting a long time in the tub?

LUDOVICA: Half an hour or so.

AZDAK: Public Prosecutor, just drop your knife on the floor. *Shauva does so.* Ludovica, go and pick up the Public Prosecutor's knife.

Ludovica, hips swaying, goes and picks up the knife.

Azdak points at her. Do you see that? The way it sways? The criminal element has been discovered. The rape has been proved. By eating too much,

especially sweet things, by lying too long in warm water, by laziness and too
soft a skin, you have raped the poor man. Do you imagine you can go around
with a bottom like that and get away with it in Court? This is a case of delib-
erate assault with a dangerous weapon. You are sentenced to hand over to
the Court the little roan that your father liked to ride on behalf of his son. And
now, Ludovica, come with me to the stable so that the Court may investigate
the scene of the crime.

(Brecht 1984, 2005: 75–7)

Method I: reading against the grain

In the essay 'Short Description of a New Technique of Acting which
Produces a Defamiliarization Effect' Brecht encourages actors to
read their parts attentively and with the attitude of someone who
'is astounded and contradicts' (*BT* 137). During rehearsals Brecht used
a variety of methods to nurture this astonished attitude. For
example, he often modified traditional read-through practice, in
which each part is played with an attempt at characterization by a
specific actor, a method that can encourage a prematurely fixed
interpretation of character and an emphasis on continuity. Instead, his
ensemble sometimes conducted a 'naive' reading, sharing parts around
the group, changing the performer when the speaker changed without
attempting to match performers to parts, and reading lightly with
interest rather than 'drama' (Leach 2004: 123). According to the diary
of directorial assistant Hans Bunge, during the first day of rehearsals
for the 1954 *Chalk Circle* there was no initial read-through at all: work
began with scene 2 (Fuegi 1987: 148). Throughout the rehearsals that
followed, scenes were rehearsed out of chronological order and as self-
contained episodes, and actors were encouraged to play without
scripts, their lines fed to them by a prompter. The sheer quantity of
these methods of segmentation indicates the extent of Brecht's interest in cultivating surprise and contradictions. In settings in which
the play is unfamiliar, however, some sort of initial read-through is
advisable in order to establish a level of familiarity – otherwise
distanciation cannot occur. What Method I offers is a version of how
to achieve a 'naive' reading, one that interrupts the text's flow and
estranges its contents so that the Brechtian quizzical attitude is
maintained.

The read-through requires five speakers, one to vocalize the stage directions and the others to take the parts of Azdak, the Innkeeper, Ludovica and the Stableman. Throughout Part 2 there should be a number of directorial assistants whose task is to describe and analyse, on paper, the unfolding rehearsal and its reception. All the other participants who are not performing should memorize their first impressions, focusing especially on phenomena that surprised, irritated and puzzled them and thereby forced them to reassess something. During the reading, the assistants underline parts of the text where the onlookers overtly express their reactions, particularly the groans and laughter that register their surprise. After the reading, first impressions are shared briefly and recorded, with speakers always prefacing their comments by 'I was surprised/astounded/puzzled by ... '. For example:

- I was surprised that judge Azdak, representative of law and order, was so sleazy.
- I was astounded by the way Azdak was more interested in the beautiful horses than the rape case he was meant to be trying.
- I was puzzled to hear that the first thing the Innkeeper did, when he discovered the Stableman 'raping' Ludovica, was to berate her on behalf of his son.
- I was surprised by the rehearsed quality of Ludovica's speech.
- I was astounded by the way Azdak turned the victim into the culprit, and the way he managed to manipulate the proceedings in order to get the result he wanted.
- I was puzzled by the fact that the authors used the sexist phrase 'voluptuous wench' to characterize Ludovica.

At this point, no one interpretation of the social meaning of the episode should be finalized. Rather it is an opportunity to air opinions and to start locating the scene's contradictions (the unlawful judge, the guilty victim) and the pivot points where the defendants become the accused.

Method II: telling the *Fabel* through partisan tableaux

For Brecht, one of the principal functions of a rehearsal was to provide a playing space for collaborative experimentation with ways of telling the *Fabel*, particularly by visual means such as **Arrangement** (the configuration and movements of the actors). In this section of Part 2, participants can experience a Brechtian approach to optical narration through the creation of partisan tableaux that illuminate not only the plot, but also the position from which it is being told.

Workshop members are divided into groups of seven, who will portray Azdak, Innkeeper, Ludovica, Stableman, Shauva, Manservant and Ironshirt. Each group creates three or four tableaux that optically narrate either Section A (up to but not including Ludovica's speech) or Section B (from her account to the end). The tableaux must tell the story from the perspective of *one* of the characters, with the WL discreetly allocating a different character to each group. Groups should begin by spelling out among themselves the interests and concerns of their character. They should then create comportments and groupings that demonstrate how that figure views other characters and events. Careful attention should be paid to the relation between all figures in each 'snapshot'. The resulting tableaux are presented and the onlookers must be able to recognize which character's perspective is being represented. If this is not clear, the tableaux should be modified.

Telling the tale from different perspectives can awaken a more informed understanding (than a simple read-through can give) of the need to explore the social conflicts played out in the scene and to express physically an attitude towards them. For example, telling the Innkeeper's tale means investigating what he means by 'family honour' and why the 'rape' of his daughter-in-law should threaten it, a concern that is hard to grasp in contemporary Western societies, where male control of property is generally less overtly enforced and infidelity more tolerated. Is he concerned that public knowledge of the 'affair', or a pregnancy, will weaken the social standing of himself and his son and threaten their livelihood and ownership of women, offspring and property? In his 1954 staging, Brecht used *Arrangement* – such as the way he had the Innkeeper stand directly behind Ludovica and whisper in her ear during her speech – to clarify that the Ensemble's *Fabel* was being told from a point of view that regarded (patriarchal) proprietorship as oppressive.

Method III: testing the gests and pivot points

When building the *Fabel* for the 1954 *Chalk Circle*, rather than imposing a pre-planned directorial concept, Brecht's approach was characterized by a playful testing of each sentence, *Gestus*, or tableau and its relation to the next one. This method kept the *Fabel* in flux, a state that Brecht prolonged by constantly suggesting new or more effective and pleasurable ways of telling the tale, even after the production had opened. In this final section of Part 2 the WL orchestrates a preliminary testing of gests and the tableaux they call forth, one that echoes Brecht's experimental and forum-oriented rehearsal process and his creation of sequences rich in oppositions and pivot points.

Some of Brecht's casting methods were informed by his interest in experimentation: the decision to cast some roles against type, to try different actors in the same part even when rehearsals were well under way, and to allow actors called in to replace an unexpectedly unavailable performer to create new attitudes and gests for the character. When casting, if workshop numbers and participant profiles allow, the WL could use some of these defamiliarizing methods. For example, an initial allocation of parts according to typecasting, or psychophysical similarity between the character and the performer, could be interrupted by an insertion of new actors cast against type for some of the roles. Such changes should be made *only if* they provide an opportunity to disrupt problematic assumptions about the *Fabel* or highlight its social commentary, and their function as potential V-effects would need to be signalled and explained.

The WL initiates this final rehearsal exercise by selecting one experienced reader as the prompter who will feed the actors' lines and be seated visibly on stage, a constant reminder of the constructed nature of the stage events. She then casts the seven characters and provides *some* rudimentary choreographing of the characters' entries and their positions during Azdak's opening lines. These can then be tested and modified through group improvisation, with the WL using questions and suggestions (rather than commands) to stimulate inventive responses from the performers. Another important goal for the WL is to ensure that actors *show* new ways of playing each line or segment rather than simply verbalize the possibilities. This approach helps performers to achieve full bodily expression of social bearing. It also makes immediately apparent the repercussions of their actions for all the players, the *Arrangement* and the *Fabel*. Take, for example, Azdak's line 'The wind blows her skirts up and you can see what's underneath' – his unexpected explanation for why 'It's good for Justice to do it in the open'. If it is played as a smutty punchline about how to get to the truth (or 'bottom') of legal matters and institutions and directed to the assembled males with a *Gestus* of collegiality, it calls forth a tableau useful for building a commentary on male control of law and order. If, by contrast, it is played as a warning that this judge takes pleasure in exposing concealment in court, and directed to the Innkeeper with a *Gestus* of cheeky provocation, it generates a stage picture that illustrates defiance of a law that is subservient to those with property.

With regard to the sequence of gests and tableaux – and there may only be time to test a few of these – it is important to build in contradictory comportments and pivot points that highlight the *Fabel*'s social meanings. Brecht's use of pivot points, interruptive moments at which a scene is given a change of direction and/or a character is given a change of behaviour, is illuminated by the way he rehearsed Ludovica's 'unveiling'. Before she gives her account, Azdak instructs her to lift her veil. Brecht suggested to the actor playing Azdak, Ernst Busch, that he speak in an indifferent tone to show that, having already eaten well and feeling lazy and tired, Azdak is uninterested in the proceedings. However, seeing how attractive Ludovica is, his indifference is abruptly replaced with lusty interest and telegraphed by his bounce up and down on his chair (BBA 944/79). Through the pivot from a *Gestus* of satiated indifference to a ridiculous *Gestus* of lusty desire, Brecht humorously signalled how a judge's decision-making process is not impartial but conditioned by fluid and material circumstances. He also began to establish a commentary on the way Azdak's deliberations would be influenced by his sexual desire for and political power over Ludovica.

Method IV: using the past to question the present

In this concluding section of the workshop, a discussion of whether and how the rape trial could be presented today is followed by a final reworking of the scene, one informed by the needs of the contemporary context. As Brecht the historicist would have asked, how can this mid-twentieth-century text with its depiction of a mythical feudal setting be staged so that it generates an inquiring attitude towards the property relations of the early twenty-first century? One starting-point could be the issue of whether the scene troublingly affirms rather than problematizes the oppressive treatment of women by men. This is how it was interpreted by the feminist critic Sara Lennox, who in the late 1970s described it as one of the worst examples of sexism in Brecht, arguing that the verdict vindicated 'a stableboy of his responsibility for rape because of the seductive appearance of his victim' (Lennox 1978: 88). But does the scene's overt display of Azdak's abuse of power simply endorse his sexism, or does it hold his behaviour, and the system of patriarchal ownership that sanctions it, up for judgement too?

This question can be profitably addressed through a return to any of the puzzling elements of the text raised during the read-through, particularly those concerning Azdak and Ludovica. Brecht is clear in his notes on the play that Azdak is a contradictory entity, a Robin Hood with selfish and amoral features. He attributes these negative behaviours to Azdak's social awareness that the new rulers of Grusinia, who in a moment of carnivalesque chaos allowed village clerk Azdak to become judge, have not really abandoned the old regime (see Chapter 3). The play demonstrates that Azdak's focus on his own pleasure, and his offensive tendency to pursue it at the expense of others, are also habits born of a lifetime spent surviving that man-made territorial warfare that dominated the old regime.

Ludovica is also characterized in relation to that social order. The use of the stock-type label 'voluptuous wench' to introduce her is a case in point. It is possible that Brecht and Co. had simply fallen prey to the mentality of sexist medieval Georgia. However, given the thoughtful treatment of women and gender concerns elsewhere in the play, and the politically correct depictions in the opening scene of female tractor drivers and agronomists in Soviet Georgia, another possibility is that the label – which in the German original is slightly derogatory – was knowingly used in order to provoke a questioning attitude towards Ludovica and her position as trophy wife and sex object. Brecht regarded this position as a common experience for wives of the propertied classes in feudal and capitalist societies. Other puzzling aspects of the scene encourage reflection on why she has been reduced to such an object. Take for example the rehearsed and comical nature of 'her' speech, which suggests the account has been concocted to suit the Innkeeper's preferred version of events. Is she the victim of rape by the stableman, and/or of a patriarchal system that positions her as a property to be controlled by the law of the father? Azdak's seemingly irrelevant questions about her eating and bathing habits also serve to raise the question of whether her acceptance of a pampered and dependent lifestyle has made her complicit in her own victimization, and possibly that of the stableman. Pursuing the source of shocks produced by the initial reading of the text illuminates a presentation of oppressive gender-power relations that is far more complex and relevant than Lennox suggests.

If the rape trial is to avoid the pitfalls either of endorsing Azdak's sexist verdict or presenting Ludovica as simply a powerless victim, the workshop ensemble needs to find ways of commenting on each figure's contribution to invidious habits of ownership. One solution, for example, might be to stage a multivocal response to Azdak's decision, with the Innkeeper and stableman expressing different types of protest and the Ironshirt applauding it with a grin or chuckle. Another might be to cast a male in the role of Ludovica, thereby signalling, through the male's overtly artificial rendition of her self-display and obedience, that the 'voluptuous wench' and luxurious consumer is a 'man-made' construct. These or other solutions can be tried out in a forum-style finale during which the WL and cast test the ongoing use-value of Brecht's legacy by responding to suggestions from the floor.

CONCLUSION

Experimenting with the exercises and rehearsal techniques outlined in this chapter should give you a better appreciation of the rousing, playful and beautifully crafted nature of Brecht's methods for encouraging us to be agents of social and artistic change. While Brecht's theatre is often caricatured in Anglo-American circles as a dull and dusty classroom experience, the arts of intervention presented here and elsewhere in this book should not leave you feeling alienated from your social world, but rather more equipped and motivated to seek out and resolve its oppressive contradictions, both on and off stage.

Grasping the legacy of Brecht and his collaborators involves exploring both a particular way of interpreting the world and how it can be expressed through theatrical means. As this chapter has demonstrated, one way of getting to know his interpretative approach is to start looking more closely – and perhaps with astonishment – at:

• your own social roles, attitudes and comportments;

- familiar behaviours, customs, relations and divisions between people;
- anything labelled 'natural' and 'eternal', in case it is actually socially constructed, historically specific and open to change.

If you want to access and understand the artistic strategies inspired by his interventionist agenda, a useful starting-point is to try out the methods outlined in this chapter, such as:

- externalizing social conditioning and power relations, particularly through framed comportment, gesture, gaze, use of props and tableaux;
- defamiliarizing the familiar through cross-casting, role doubling and the opposition of imitation and stylization, **empathy** and demonstration;
- maintaining a quizzical attitude by means of an experimental segmented approach that interrupts the flow of text and action; and
- signalling changeability through 'fixing the "not-but"', contradictory gests and sequences rich with pivot points.

Once you have really begun to inhabit a theatre practice inspired by Brecht you will feel as if you are in the middle of an energized playground, one that cultivates the passionate wit, transformative imagination and sense of justice that are so crucial to the social art of pleasurable production.

GLOSSARY

agitprop Agitprop is a type of political theatre that uses bold rhetorical techniques to inform and mobilize its audience about urgent social issues. Its name derives from the Department of Agitation and Propaganda established in 1920 by the Soviet Communist Party. While agitprop theatre has been used in many different times and places, it was particularly prominent during the interwar years in Europe, where it was associated with Marxist politics. Brecht reworked many characteristic features of the form, including: episodic structure, sloganistic banners, mass chants, heroic tableaux, satire, emblematic scenography, direct address and audience participation. While agitprop tends to instruct its audience about the way forward in a forceful and often reductive manner, Brecht's theatre invites the spectator to develop a problem-solving attitude towards a complex and contradictory world.

alienation Following Marx, Brecht held the assumption that labour power – the capacity to transform nature – was a fundamental aspect of human nature. Furthermore, he agreed that the removal of the workers' ownership of their labour power under capitalism had caused alienation from self and fellow worker. Rather than enjoying their own creativity and ability to satisfy the needs of others, labourers were reduced to machines and commodities for whom work was a disempowering activity that perpetuated exploitation. In his theatre Brecht used various

Verfremdung or defamiliarization strategies to expose alienation as a historical, man-made phenomenon, and to rouse spectators to use their capacity to control and transform their lives and social relations.

Aristotelian This was the classificatory adjective that Brecht applied to Western dramaturgy and performance that he rejected as idealist, fatalist and psychologizing. Brecht associated this dominant tradition with the dramatic theories of the ancient Greek philosopher Aristotle (384–c. 322 BC). Speaking from the perspective of a historical materialist, Brecht claimed that the Aristotelian tradition was underpinned by ideas and practices that impeded social revolution. These included: the idealist notion that consciousness determines human being; the fatalist idea that human nature is unalterable and given at birth; and the universalizing tendency to downplay social difference and promote instead humankind's shared 'common humanity'. Brecht also argued that these ideas were embodied in dramaturgical devices, such as an uninterrupted linear dovetailing of events that focused attention on the unfolding of the protagonist's given destiny. The aspect of Aristotelian performance that he regarded as particularly ill-suited to a revolutionary agenda – because it reproduced the familiar and presented it as given and eternal – was its emphasis on imitation and associated psychological processes such as empathy and catharsis. Against this 'dramatic theatre' of present-tense, dialogue-based drama, Brecht pitted a dialectical epic theatre, which interrupted the drama with narrative commentary and illuminated the world as a construct open to change.

Arrangement The term Brecht used during rehearsal to describe a dynamic and socially significant type of sculptural choreography. An *Arrangement* is the live composition of groupings, gestures and movements that vividly elucidates the events, the psychosocial position and relations of the characters, and the contradictions of the depicted social world in a particular episode or scene.

bourgeoisie and *petite bourgeoisie* Marx used the term 'bourgeoisie' to refer to the legal owners of merchant, industrial and money capital who, by the nineteenth century, had replaced the aristocracy as the ruling class in control of the means of production (including land, factories, capital, labour power etc.), and hence the state and cultural apparatus. Today the term is also applied to high-powered managers and government officials who may not legally own capital but who have considerable control over it. In accordance with Marxist thought, Brecht regarded the bourgeoisie as in opposition to and exploitative of the proletariat. Marx named the intermediate group between these two antagonistic classes the 'middle class'. This diverse group encompasses workers with a degree of economic independence (e.g. owners of small businesses) and those who, while they have only limited control of capital, may buy the labour power of others (e.g. professionals). Frequently the terms 'middle class' and 'bourgeoisie' are used interchangeably. However, in Marxist parlance only significant owners or controllers of capital can be classified as belonging to the bourgeoisie. Brecht often called members of the 'middle class' – particularly small-business and property owners – the *petite bourgeoisie*.

capitalism A mode of production that emerged in feudal Europe between the fifteenth and eighteenth centuries whose central feature is the private ownership of capital by the bourgeois ruling class. Here 'capital' means not simply assets that generate income for their owner and enhance the development of productive forces such as technology, but assets that are born of and reproduce coercive social relations and an inequitable private property system. Marx argued that the starting point for capitalist society was the removal of serfdom and of the guilds' restrictive labour regulations, which led to the entry *en masse* of peasants and apprentices into the labour market where they were 'free' to sell their capacity to work. Unlike other commodities, these new wage labourers had the ability to produce goods and services that could be sold for a higher sum than both their wage (which covered their maintenance and reproduction costs) and the other costs of the production process put together. That is, they could be used to generate surplus value and ensure their employer's accumulation of capital. Marx theorized that in the competitive free market, capitalists would be forced to cut pay to maintain profit, which would ultimately contribute to a proletarian uprising, the overthrow of capitalism, and the advent of communism.

class   According to Marx, an economic class comprises a group of people defined by their role in the mode of production. The ruling class is the group which has economic ownership or significant control of the *forces* and *relations* of production (see **historical materialism**). By contrast, the working class or proletariat is the group which must sell their capacity to work and who have no ownership of the means of production.

comportment   In this book 'comportment' is the portmanteau term used to mean the social 'bearing', 'carriage', 'posture' and 'attitude' of the fictional character and/or the theatre practitioner. It has been selected as the preferred translation of the German word '*Haltung*', the term Brecht used to describe an important aspect of his theory and practice of *Gestus*. Usually *Haltung* is translated as 'attitude', which in English connotes mental response and psychological disposition. However, when Brecht used *Haltung* he was referring both to a mental stance *and* a body orientation. 'Comportment' better elucidates Brecht's interest in the interdependency of mind and matter, and in demonstrating the socially conditioned relation to time, space and people of a thinking body.

defamiliarization   See *Verfremdung*.

dialectics   In classical philosophy, dialectics or the dialectical method is a mode of resolving disagreement and furthering knowledge that involves pitting theses, or propositions, against antitheses. Brecht's interest in the dialectical play of opposites as a tool for understanding permeates his use of defamiliarizing strategies such as: the juxtaposition of contemporary demonstrator-performer and historical character; the 'not-but' method, which involves playing a character's action and simultaneously indicating what the character is *not* doing; the staging of visual oppositions and contradictory actions; and the collision of naturalness and stylization, empathic understanding and analytical demonstration.

dialectical materialism   Dialectical materialism, the philosophical basis of Marxism, combines a dialectical belief in the transformative power of opposition with a materialist idea of history as progressive development brought about by human labour and class struggle (see **historical materialism**). Not only do the plots and characters of Brecht's plays illuminate the struggle between ruling class and proletariat, but some of his techniques embody the workings of the dialectical laws of development outlined by Marx's collaborator, Friedrich Engels. For instance, Brecht's scripting of contradictory actions (e.g. Mother Courage damning war in one scene and praising it in the very next) embodies the law of the unity of opposites according to which everything in existence is an unstable unity of two mutually incompatible but indispensable parts, and hence capable of movement and change. For a fuller discussion of the theatrical embodiment of these laws, see the section on dialectics in Chapter 2.

dramatic theatre   See **Aristotelian**.

empathy   While the meaning of 'empathy' varies depending on context and historical period, it commonly denotes a psychological process that involves imagining or experiencing the thoughts and feelings of another. Empathic understanding occurs when the observer experiences a state of mind similar to that of the person being observed, a situation that arises if the observer has some understanding of the other person's circumstances and has had analogous feelings. The empathic observer engages in voluntary analogical thinking which helps her to become familiar and close to the observed while simultaneously remaining aware of her separateness (e.g. 'I think I understand much of the way that sixteenth-century peasant woman feels because, although I haven't been browbeaten by Protestant clergy, I did experience Nazi indoctrination during the Second World War'). Towards the end of his career Brecht promoted a dialectical approach to acting, one that combined empathic understanding with analytical demonstration. He also acknowledged that processes he associated with empathy, such as identification (modelling the self on and merging with a desired other), could occasionally be put to good use in his theatre. For example, he welcomed the spectator's identification with the analytical actor-demonstrator, and with characters engaged in active resistance such as Kattrin during the drumming scene in *Mother Courage and Her Children*. However, Brecht maintained a life-long wariness of other psychological processes such as projection, which involve actors and spectators attributing aspects of their own self and experience to others ('That's just how I would act, that peasant woman is me!'). For Brecht, such ahistorical self-reproduction inhibited awareness of the impermanent nature of the social world, and of how we, too, might be capable of change.

epic theatre 'Epic theatre' is the umbrella phrase Brecht used to describe all the technical devices and methods of interpretation that contribute to the creation of an artistic social(ist) commentary and engaged spectActor. The term 'epic' recalls the ancient genre of the long narrative poem which dealt with subjects such as national history and which was recited by a solo performer. This mode of literature and performance *tells* something about the people's past as opposed to *showing* it in present-tense, dialogue-based form. Brecht began regularly referring to his theory and practice as 'epic theatre' in the mid-1920s, a time when many artists in the Weimar Republic were using the epic mode as a vehicle for utilitarian social commentary. Brecht appropriated not only the ancient epic's narrator figure and emphasis on reportage, but also its episodic structure that he used to create astonishing juxtapositions that illuminated the contradictions and changeability of humankind. In the early 1950s Brecht announced that it was time to discard the phrase 'epic theatre', for, while it had helped reinstate narrative commentary, it had also become a formal concept associated with an inflexible opposition to dramatic theatre. From his new vantage point, the phrase 'dialectical theatre' appeared better suited to conveying the politics, content and form of his work.

Fabel Brecht used the term *Fabel* (or 'fable') to refer both to the original composition of incidents in a play text, and to its interpretational retelling on stage by socially engaged theatre practitioners who develop the interactions between characters with an eye to contradictions. For him the interpretational *Fabel* was the heart of the theatrical production.

Formalism Initially this term was applied by advocates of Soviet Socialist Realism to art they deemed to be obsessed with form at the expense of content. However, increasingly it was also used to dismiss art that deviated from their preferred model of realism, leading to the absurd situation where Marxist practitioners such as Brecht found themselves having to defend their own versions of socialist realism against accusations of Formalism.

Gestus **(pl. gests)** From the late 1920s onwards, Brecht used the Latin word *Gestus* to mean one or all of the following: social(ized) gesticulation as opposed to psychological facial expression; contextualized and alterable comportment; and the rhetorical artistic gestures of a performer. For the theatre practitioner, showing a *Gestus* involved crafting gestures, comportments and groupings so that they vividly illuminated the way human behaviour and social relations are both shaped by economic and historical forces, and open to change.

historical materialism According to historical materialism, the Marxist conception of history, what distinguishes humans from other animals is their capacity to produce the means of their subsistence, and to do so through a process of conscious collaboration and innovation. This capacity gives rise to the mode of production which historical materialists regard as the moving force behind the progressive development of society. A mode of production is a socio-economic system comprising both *forces* of production (e.g. land, natural resources, technology, labour power) and *relations* of production (arrangements regarding who does and who owns what). Marx argued – and this theory is much debated within Marxist circles – that social revolution occurs when new productive forces (e.g. industrial machinery) come into conflict with old relations of production (e.g. under feudalism, serfs were tied to land and lord and prohibited from becoming the very wage earners industry requires). The ensuing struggle for power between the old and emergent owners of production (e.g. the landowning aristocracy and bourgeois industrialists) is resolved through the establishment of a new mode of production (e.g. capitalism). Each revolution or stage in history – from primitive communism, through slave society, feudalism, and capitalism, to the 'higher phase' of communism – is progressive in so far as it ushers in a society with a greater productive capacity, setting the conditions for human liberation from divisive competition for resources. Brecht presents a vision of the early stages of a communist society free from antagonistic division in the opening scene of *The Caucasian Chalk Circle* (see Chapter 3). While utopian episodes such as these are rare in Brecht's *oeuvre*, other aspects of historical materialist thought feature prominently in his post-1926 theatre, especially the idea that human behaviour and interaction are determined in the first instance not by an inborn consciousness, but by the way we produce and reproduce ourselves.

historicization 'Historicization' is the term Brecht used to describe artistic defamiliarizing strategies – referred to in this book as 'H-effects' – designed to provoke an inquiring attitude towards the present through the past, and challenge dominant versions of history. Historicization can involve: presenting an event as the product of historically specific (rather than eternal) material conditions and human choices; showing the differences between past and present in order to highlight change; showing the problematic continuities between past and present in order to prompt change; and foregrounding the partisan and ideological nature of any writing or other telling of history. Brecht's historicist approach is guided by the Marxist conception of history. See **historical materialism**.

ideology Marx defined 'ideology' as both: (1) the consciousness (or ways of thinking and feeling) associated with the members of an economic class and their productive activities; and (2) a consciousness that supports the ruling class. An example of the first approach to ideology can be found in Brecht's staging of the episode in *The Tutor* where the Maid ushers in Count Wermuth to the von Bergs' home. Her impassioned tone and inability to remove her eyes from the elegant Count was intended to convey the type of admiring and subservient attitude towards the oppressor that was typical of many servants trapped in a situation of economic dependence. The second approach to ideology informs the episode in Brecht's play *Life of Galileo*, where impoverished fairground performers sing a ballad about the way the seventeenth-century clergy's advocacy of the Ptolemaic theory of the universe – according to which the earth is central, with all other celestial bodies, such as the sun and fixed stars, revolving around it – serves to bolster a pope-centred hierarchical society.

Lehrstück Between 1926 and 1933 Brecht and his collaborators wrote a series of *Lehrstücke* ('learning-plays'), including well-known texts such as *The Mother*, *The Measures Taken*, *He Who Said Yes* and *He Who Said No*. Unlike the *Schaustücke* ('show/showing plays'), which were designed to be subversive presentations to the passive consumers of mainstream capitalist theatre, Brecht conceived the *Lehrstücke* as material for producers. In particular, they were targeted at participants involved in effecting the transition to socialism, be they the pupils at the Karl Marx School in Berlin-Neuköln during the Weimar Republic, or the founders of socialist East Germany. Brecht's radical *Lehrstück* theory was that the copying and correction of a character's behaviours in an ethically complex social scenario would give performers an opportunity to rehearse interventionist thought and action. While Brecht took an active involvement in *Schaustück* stagings of the plays, his focus remained their function as experiential pedagogy for performers. Many influential practitioners since Brecht have been inspired by this pedagogy, most notably the Brazilian performance maker and politician Augusto Boal (b. 1931).

Modellbuch The 'model book' was both an educational tool and an innovative archive method – in an age prior to video documentation – that was designed to assist dissemination of Brecht's post-1945 methods of staging. Pioneered by Brecht's collaborator Ruth Berlau, each production report consisted of black and white photos and explanatory notes detailing the *Gestus*-oriented approach to character as well as the *Arrangement* of the *Fabel*. In the chaotic period immediately after the Second World War, where Brecht was often forced to do battle with the legacy of Nazi performance and the promoters of Soviet-inspired cultural policy, the model books proved a useful method for introducing and protecting his practice. Brecht often put considerable pressure on both outside directors wishing to stage his plays and members of the Berliner Ensemble dramaturgical team to consult the relevant model books. However, he cautioned against mindless copying, encouraging reflective and corrective imitation instead. Quite a number of the production compilations were published in the 1950s, and three of these, together with previously unpublished *Katzgraben* notes, appear in volume 25 of the most recent edition of Brecht's writings. An English-language translation of the *Courage* model book (minus the photographs) is available in volume 5 of *Collected Plays* (Brecht 1972: 334–86).

proletariat   The proletariat, or working class, are those workers who have no ownership or control of the means of production. Marx regarded the proletariat as the revolutionary material force that would bring about the destruction of capitalism and transition to socialism. Two factors in particular qualified the nineteenth-century European proletariat for this role: first, their subjection to intense deprivation and alienation gave them good cause to revolt; and second, industrialization had increased their number and led to their concentration in greater masses, making it possible for them to become a formidable united opponent to the bourgeoisie. Recent developments in capitalist countries, such as the welfare state and the growth of the middle class (see the entry on the **bourgeoisie**), have necessitated the emergence of new theories about the role of the proletariat in the liberation of humankind from alienation.

Socialist Realism   'Socialist Realism' is a label most commonly applied to the prescribed artistic practice that emerged from the First Congress of the Union of Soviet Writers in 1934, and to derivative forms such as the approach to literature and performance promoted by the East German arbiters of culture during the early 1950s. The German model continued the Soviet emphasis on intelligible art free from abstractions. Its proponents eschewed the overt didacticism and experimentation that had characterized the revolutionary workers' art traditions during the Weimar Republic, and advocated instead the development of bourgeois realism and its tradition of uninterrupted illusionism. Brecht's decision to call his work 'socialist realist' was a provocative assertion of an alternative political aesthetic. His version of realism embodied the conviction that formal experimentation was crucial to the pleasurable and historically specific *mastery (as opposed to mere reproduction) of contradictory social reality.*

spectActor   In this book the term 'spectActor' is used as a playful descriptor for both the type of actor Brecht's theatre requires, and the type of spectator he sought to cultivate. The Brechtian performer is a spectActor in so far as s/he must 'act out' or imitate the actions, thoughts and feelings of the character to be portrayed, as well as critically watching and demonstrating their behaviour from a socially engaged perspective. The actor-cum-commentator in turn reminds the audience that they too are capable of adopting an activist approach to the stage and social world; that is, the spectator is encouraged to be a reflective interventionist. Here the Brechtian spectActor meets the 'spect-actor' of Augusto Boal's Theatre of the Oppressed. What distinguishes Boal's spectator is that s/he also enters the action on stage, either through verbal means or by literally walking onto the playing space and changing a character's actions and the events of the play. Brecht's theatre usually maintains a physical separation of actor and spectator, with the latter remaining in the auditorium, although the **Lehrstück** participant provides a notable exception.

Verfremdung and **V-effect** Verfremdung is a German word coined by Brecht and used to refer to artistic strategies that both arouse new insights into concealed or overly familiar social phenomena, and initiate problem-solving activism. Brecht often referred to these strategies as 'V-effects'. Examples include: making the lighting apparatus, musicians and set changes visible so that human labour power is put on full display; interrupting the flow of action through the insertion of narration, songs and direct address which draw attention to the social causes of the events; and generating a split between the contemporary actor-demonstrator and the historical character which illuminates the historical and changeable nature of humankind. Brecht began using the term after he became interested in Marx's theory of *Entfremdung* ('alienation'). However, to translate *Verfremdung* as 'alienation' is misleading for at least two reasons. First, while Brecht certainly used V-effects to reveal systematic alienation under capitalism, this was only one of the thematic concerns they were applied to. And second, the term 'alienation' encourages the misinterpretation that Brecht sought a separation of actor, character and spectator that mimicked rather than subverting the hostilities of alienation. In this book the preferred translation is 'defamiliarization', a word that conveys his desire to illuminate the (blindingly) familiar status quo.

BIBLIOGRAPHY

Bathrick, David (1990) 'Max Schmeling on the Canvas: Boxing as an Icon of Weimar Culture', *New German Critique* 51, pp. 113–36.

Berg-Pan, Renata (1975) 'Mixing Old and New Wisdom: The "Chinese" Sources of Brecht's *Kaukasischer Kreidekreis* and Other Works', *German Quarterly* 48, pp. 204–28.

Bishop, Philip E. (1986) 'Brecht, Hegel, Lacan: Brecht's Theory of Gest and the Problem of the Subject', *Studies in Twentieth Century Literature* 10: 2, pp. 267–88.

Bradley, Laura (2006) *Brecht and Political Theatre: The Mother on Stage*, Oxford: Clarendon.

Brecht, Bertolt (1964) 'Notes on Stanislavski', trans. Carl R. Mueller, *Tulane Drama Review* 9: 2, pp. 155–66.

—— (1965) *The Messingkauf Dialogues*, trans. John Willett, London: Methuen.

—— (1967) 'BB's Rehearsal Scenes – Estranging Shakespeare', *The Drama Review* 12: 1, pp. 108–11.

—— (1972) *Collected Plays*, vol. 5, eds Ralph Manheim and John Willett, New York: Vintage.

—— (1976) *Collected Plays*, vol. 7, eds John Willett and Ralph Manheim, London: Eyre Methuen.

—— (1978) *Brecht on Theatre: The Development of an Aesthetic*, ed. and trans. John Willett, New York: Hill and Wang; London: Methuen.

—— (1979a) *Collected Plays*, vol. 2i, ed. and trans. John Willett and Ralph Manheim, London: Eyre Methuen.

—— (1979b) *Diaries 1920–22*, ed. Herta Ramthun, trans. John Willett, London: Eyre Methuen.

—— (1979c) *Poems*, ed. and trans. John Willett and Ralph Manheim, 2nd edn, London: Eyre Methuen.

—— (1984, 2005) *The Caucasian Chalk Circle*, trans. James and Tania Stern with W.H. Auden, London: Methuen.

—— (1986) *Life of Galileo*, trans. John Willett, London: Methuen.

—— (1990) *Letters 1913–1956*, trans. Ralph Manheim and ed. John Willett, London: Methuen.

—— (1991) *Werke: Große kommentierte Berliner und Frankfurter Ausgabe*, vol. 24, eds Peter Kraft et al., Berlin and Frankfurt am Main: Aufbau and Suhrkamp.

—— (1992) *Werke: Große kommentierte Berliner und Frankfurter Ausgabe*, vol. 8, ed. Klaus-Detlef Müller, Berlin and Frankfurt am Main: Aufbau and Suhrkamp.

—— (1993) *Journals*, trans. Hugh Rorrison, ed. John Willett, London: Methuen.

—— (1998) *Collected Plays*, vol. 1, eds John Willett and Ralph Manheim, London: Methuen.

—— (1999) *The Caucasian Chalk Circle*, English version by Eric Bentley, Minneapolis: The University of Minnesota Press.

—— (2001) *Brecht on Film and Radio*, ed. and trans. Marc Silberman, London: Methuen.

—— (2003) *Brecht on Art and Politics*, eds Tom Kuhn and Steve Giles, London: Methuen.

Brooker, Peter (1988) *Bertolt Brecht: Dialectics, Poetry and Politics*, London: Croom Helm.

Bryant-Bertail, Sarah (2000) *Space and Time in Epic Theater: The Brechtian Legacy*, New York: Camden.

Calandra, Denis (1974) 'Karl Valentin and Bertolt Brecht', *The Drama Review* 18: 1, pp. 86–98.

Dickson, Keith (1978) *Towards Utopia: A Study of Brecht*, Oxford: Clarendon.

Dieckmann, Friedrich (ed.) (1971) *Karl von Appens Bühnenbilder am Berliner Ensemble*, Berlin: Henschel, Kunst und Gesellschaft.

Eddershaw, Margaret (1991) 'Echt Brecht? "Mother Courage" at the Citizens, 1990', *New Theatre Quarterly* 7: 28, pp. 303–14.

Evenden, Michael (1986) 'Beyond Verfremdung: Notes Toward a Brecht "Theaterturgy"' in *Before his Eyes: Essays in Honor of Stanley Kauffmann*, ed. Bert Cardullo, Lanham, MD: University Press of America.

Ewen, Frederic (1970) *Bertolt Brecht. His Life, His Art and His Times*, London: Calder and Boyars.

Fogg, Derek (1991) '*Mother Courage and Her Children*, by Bertolt Brecht' in *The Citizens' Theatre Season: Glasgow 1990*, eds Jan McDonald and Claude Schumacher, Glasgow: Theatre Studies Publications.

Fuegi, John (1987) *Bertolt Brecht: Chaos, According to Plan*, Cambridge: Cambridge University Press.

Giles, Steve (1997) *Bertolt Brecht and Critical Theory: Marxism, Modernity and the Threepenny Lawsuit*, Bern: Peter Lang.

Hecht, Werner (1966) *Materialien zu Brechts 'Der Kaukasische Kreidekreis'*, Frankfurt am Main: Suhrkamp.

Hecht, Werner (ed.) (1985) *Brechts Theaterarbeit. Seine Inszenierung des 'Kaukasischen Kreidekreises' 1954*, Frankfurt am Main: Suhrkamp.

Hurwicz, Angelika (1964) *Brecht inszeniert: Der kaukasische Kreidekreis*, photos by Gerda Goedhart, Velber bei Hannover: Erhard Friedrich.

Jones, David Richard (1986) *Great Directors at Work: Stanislavsky, Brecht, Kazan, Brook*, Berkeley: University of California Press.

Kinzer, Craig (1991) 'Brecht, the "Fabel", and the Teaching of Directing', *The Brecht Yearbook* 16, pp. 25–37.

Leach, Robert (2004) *Makers of Modern Theatre: An Introduction*, London and New York: Routledge.

Lennox, Sara (1978) 'Women in Brecht's Works', *New German Critique* 14, pp. 83–96.

Lyon, James K. (1980) *Bertolt Brecht in America*, London: Methuen.

—— (1999) 'Elements of American Theatre and Film in Brecht's *Caucasian Chalk Circle*', *Modern Drama* 42: 2, pp. 238–46.

McDowell, W. Stuart (1976) 'Actors on Brecht: The Munich Years', *The Drama Review* 20: 3, pp. 101–16.

Martin, Carol (2000) 'Brecht, Feminism, and Chinese Theatre' in *Brecht Sourcebook*, ed. Carol Martin and Henry Bial, London: Routledge, pp. 228–36.

Marx, Karl (1977) *Selected Writings*, ed. D. McLellan, Oxford: Oxford University Press.

Mitter, Shomit (1992) *Systems of Rehearsal: Stanislavsky, Brecht, Grotowski and Brook*, London and New York: Routledge.

Mumford, Meg (1995) 'Brecht Studies Stanislavski: Just a Tactical Move?', *New Theatre Quarterly* 11: 43, pp. 241–58.

—— (1998) ' "Dragging Brecht's Gestus Onwards": A Feminist Challenge' in *Bertolt Brecht: Centenary Essays*, eds Steve Giles and Rodney Livingstone, Amsterdam: Rodopi, pp. 240–57.

—— (2001) 'Gestic Masks in Brecht's Theater: A Testimony to the Contradictions and Parameters of a Realist Aesthetic', *The Brecht Yearbook* 26, pp. 143–71.

—— (2003) 'Verfremdung' in *The Oxford Encyclopedia of Theatre and Performance*, vol. 2, ed. Dennis Kennedy, Oxford: Oxford University Press, pp. 1404–5.

Nussbaum, Laureen (1993) 'Brecht's Revised Version of Genesis 1 and 2: A Subtext of the *Caucasian Chalk Circle*', *Communications from the International Brecht Society* 22: 1, pp. 41–50.

Philpotts, Matthew (2003) '"Aus so prosaischen Dingen wie Kartoffeln, Straßen, Traktoren werden poetische Dinge!": Brecht, *Sinn und Form*, and Strittmatter's *Katzgraben*', *German Life and Letters* 56: 1, pp. 56–71.

Ramthun, Herta (ed.) (1969–73) *Bertolt-Brecht-Archiv: Bestandsverzeichnis des literarischen Nachlasses*, 4 vols, Berlin and Weimar: Aufbau.

Rouse, John (1984) 'Brecht and the Contradictory Actor', *Theatre Journal* 36: 1, pp. 25–41.

—— (1989) *Brecht and the West German Theatre: The Practice and Politics of Interpretation*, Ann Arbor, MI: U.M.I. Research Press.

Schumacher, Ernst and Renate Schumacher (1981), *Leben Brechts in Wort und Bild*, Berlin: Henschel.

Speirs, Ronald (1982) 'Brecht in the German Democratic Republic' in *Brecht in Perspective*, eds Graham Bartram and Anthony Waine, London: Longman, pp. 175–89.

Subiotto, Arrigo (1975) *Bertolt Brecht's Adaptations for the Berliner Ensemble*, London: MHRA.

Suvin, Darko (1989) 'Brecht's *Caucasian Chalk Circle* and Marxist Figuralism: Open Dramaturgy as Open History' in *Critical Essays on Bertolt Brecht*, ed. Siegfried Mews, Boston, MA: G.K. Hall.

Taylor, Ronald (ed.) (1977) *Aesthetics and Politics*, London: NLB.

Thomson, Peter and Glendyr Sacks (eds) (1994) *The Cambridge Companion to Brecht*, Cambridge: Cambridge University Press.

Tynan, Kenneth (1976) '*The Caucasian Chalk Circle*, *Mother Courage* and *Trumpets and Drums* at the Palace' (1956) in Kenneth Tynan, *A View of the English Stage*, Frogmore, St Albans, Herts: Paladin.

Völker, Klaus (1979) *Brecht: A Biography*, trans. John Newell, London: Calder and Boyars.

Weber, Carl (1967) 'Brecht as Director', *The Drama Review* 12: 1, pp. 101–7.

White, Alfred D. (1978) *Bertolt Brecht's Great Plays*, London and Basingstoke: Macmillan.

Willett, John (1977) *The Theatre of Bertolt Brecht: A Study from Eight Aspects*, rev. edn, London: Methuen.

INDEX

as cabaret performer 13, *13*; commentaries 48–49, 51–53, 55–59; contestatory nature 7, 9; death and burial 46–47; directorial style 14, 15; education 4, 5–6; exiled 27–30, 32–36, 65, 76, 101, 131; finances 33; First World War work 6; in GDR 37–47; and Great Depression 25–27; heart condition 6; importance of flux to 1–2, 20–21, 52, 84, 90, 161; influences 12–14, 22–23, 46, 59, 102; interest in boxing 16–18, *17*; letters 40, 42, 103; lovers, wives and children 7, 8, 20, 27, 32; macho posturing 16; Marxist studies 20–22; materialism 8; medical career 6–7; one of 'Hollywood nineteen' 35–36; opposition to war 41–42; partisan approach 27, 48, 54, 63, 75–76, 106; playfulness 48, 51–52; poetry 4, 7, 28, 32–33, 41, 134–35; prizes 12, 42; promotes use of theatre in resolving disputes 103–4; 'proof of the pudding' proverb 51, 126; radio talk (1927) 18; reaction to Nazi rally 11–12; reaction to strike in GDR 39–40; remains committed to Marxism 28; role in Bavarian Republic 9–11; takes Austrian citizenship 37; theatre reviews 10; theatrical posts 14, 15; and 'think-tank' collectives 7–8, 15; in USA 30, 32–36, 93; wide scope of writings 48; *see also specific works*
Brecht, Walter (brother) 2, *3*, 4, 10
'Brecht collective' 18, 26, 29, 31, 32; *see also* Berliner Ensemble
Brecht on Theatre: The Development of an Aesthetic (*ed.* Willett) 52–53, 79, 133
Bronnen, Arnolt 11–12; *Vatermord* 14
Brueghel, Pieter 46; *Dulle Griet* 119
Bunge, Hans 92, 94, 103, 114, 117, 158
Busch, Ernst 106, 108, 120, 162

cabaret 13–14, *13*
capitalism 16, 29, 33, 47, 62, 67, 71, 75, 86, 168; depicted in plays 23–24, 68, 69; Marx on 20, 21–22, 28
Caucasian Chalk Circle, The 29, 30, 91–129, *97*, *99*; *Arrangements* 108, 109, 113–17, 125; Azdak's character and behaviour 120–22; cheese ceremony 95, 104; contradictions 116–18; costumes 111, 112; criticisms of 126–27; ending 99, 103–4; as epic 91, 104–8; epilogue 98–99; *Fabel* 109–10, 111, 113, 114, 117, 122, 125, 156–64; gender relations in 114, 115, 120–21; *Gestus* in 109, 113, 118–21, 124, 128, 160–62; Grusha's character and behaviour 118–19; Grusha's visit to Lavrenti and Aniko 121, 124–25; as historicization 100–104; influenced by American film and theatre 102; length and cost 96; lovers' 'reunion' 107–8; masks 89, 96, 105, 121, 122–26, *123*; milk-buying episode 117–18; modern productions 127–28; music 96, 103, 105–6, 112–3, 124; Natella/Shalva relationship 113–14; Natella's departure 96, 113; origins of chalk circle imagery and motherhood test 100–101; plot 95–100; Prologue (frame play/valley scene) 93–94, 100, 101, 103–5, 127–28, 172; rape trial 108, 120–21, 156–64; rehearsals for *45*, 109–10; role of Nephew 114; scenography 111–13, 120, 124, 125–26, 127; Singer 96, 106–9; soldiers 121, 122; songs 96, 99–100, 102, 105; source materials 93–95; success 126; wedding 7, 114–16, *115*, 125; workshop based on 156–64
Caucasus 95, 101, 105, 125
change 50–51; *see also* flux
Chaplin, Charlie 14, 54, 102
Chinese culture 112; theatre 59, 61, 108

Robert Lepage

Routledge Performance Practitioners series

Aleksandar Saša Dundjerović

All books in the *Routledge Performance Practitioners* series are carefully designed to enable the reader to understand the work of a key practitioner. They provide the first step towards critical understanding and a springboard for further study for students on twentieth century, contemporary theatre and theatre history courses.

Robert Lepage is one of Canada's most foremost playwrights and directors. His company – *Ex Machina* – have toured to international acclaim and he has leant his talents to areas as diverse as opera, concert tours, acting and installation art. His most celebrated work blends acute personal narratives with bold global themes.

This is the first book to combine:

- an overview of the key phases in Lepage's life and career;
- examination of the key questions pertinent to his work;
- discussion of *The Seven Streams of River Ota* as a paradigm of his working methods; and
- a variety of practical exercises designed to give an insight into Lepage's creative process.

ISBN13: 978-0-415-37519-1 (hbk)
ISBN13: 978-0-415-37520-7 (pbk)

Available at all good bookshops
For ordering and further information please visit:
www.routledge.com